Squeeze the Most Out of Your Money:

A No-Nonsense Money Management System to Maximize Your Dollars and Minimize Your Money Stress

Patricia Stallworth

iWorth Publishing
Johns Creek, Georgia

Library of Congress Cataloging-in-Publication Data is available.

ISBN: 978-0-9785502-7-1

iWorth books are available at special discounts when purchased in bulk for premiums and sales promotions as well as for fund raising or educational use. Special editions or book excerpts also can be created to specification. For details contact the Special Sales Director at the address below.

iWorth Publishing
Johns Creek, Georgia
info@iworthpublishing.com

Printed in the United States of America

First printing June 2011

This book is designed to provide accurate and authoritative information on the subject of personal finances. While all of the stories and anecdotes described in this book are based on true experiences, most of the names are pseudonyms, and some situations have been changed slightly to protect each individual's privacy. It is sold with the understanding that neither the Author nor the Publisher is engaged in rendering legal, accounting, or other professional services by publishing this book. As each individual situation is unique, questions relevant to personal finances and specific to the individual should be addressed to an appropriate professional to ensure that the situation has been evaluated carefully and appropriately. The Author and Publisher specifically disclaim any liability, loss, or risk which is incurred as a consequence, directly or indirectly, of the use and application of any of the contents of this work.

DEDICATION

I would like to say a special thank you to all of my friends and family who supported me during the writing of *Squeeze*. I have often compared writing a book to giving birth to a baby and this book was no exception, including the occasional mood swings and the odd cravings for pickles and ice cream.

I would also like to thank all of my 'old' and 'new' friends who gave so much to this book by participating in focus groups and sharing their stories, and to my colleagues who gave so freely of themselves and continuously encouraged me to keep going.

Thank you so much. I dedicate this book to you!

CONTENTS

12 Money Principles

#1: Money is just not good at managing itself so don't let it. Take control and make it work for you! (p. 11)

#2: Throwing more money at problems isn't always the answer. Squeeze your money first. Then look to other options! (p. 33)

#3: Living within your means will keep you out of debt. Living beneath your means could make you rich! (p. 47)

#4: A credit limit does not represent money you have available, so resist the temptation to act like it does! (p. 65)

#5: Stress your money, not yourself. Always keep a stash of cash on hand in case of an emergency! (p. 71)

#6: Savings are an essential part of every plan. Without them you're doomed to live in an endless loop of ESS (earning, spending, and stressing) with no end in sight! (p. 81)

#7: Including checks and balances in your spending plan allows you to self-correct and always stay in control! (p. 105)

#8: Knowing what you own and what you owe is crucial before you add to either list! (p. 135)

#9: The best way to ensure that you get to where you want to go is to develop a plan and follow it. Anything less could lead you down a totally different path! (p. 153)

#10: Investing is not just for the wealthy—it's also for those who want to get that way so get started sooner rather than later! (p. 179)

#11: Your credit score can add/subtract thousands of dollars to/from your pockets over your lifetime. Always know yours and how it affects you in dollars and cents! (p. 217)

#12: Don't let debt determine your destiny. If you're in too deep make a plan to get out. Every dollar you spend on debt today is a dollar you won't have to enjoy or invest for tomorrow! (p. 241)

SQUEEZE STORY:

Stephanie and Ron

Ron and I have been married for three years and we can't seem to get on the same page when it comes to money. Things were going along fine until we had our first child and then everything changed. Up until then we both had separate accounts, and we contributed to a household account and Ron basically paid the bills. However, I had a really difficult pregnancy and had to leave work for almost six months. During that time, I admit it, even though I didn't contribute anything to the household bills, I continued to spend like I always did, and that angered Ron who had to carry the entire household burden. In one of our counseling sessions he called it "frivolous" spending. Well I don't think it was really frivolous. Those where things that both the baby and I needed. I didn't know it but I guess I used up all of our savings. But that's not the point. The point is that money is ruining our marriage. We can't agree on anything, not even how and when to pay the bills. We decided to put all of our money into one account to simplify things, but that is just not working. Late fees and interest are racking up, and checks are bouncing all over the place because no one is keeping up with the day-to-day stuff. Ron is so angry I don't think he cares anymore, and I don't know what to do. I love my husband, but I don't know how much longer we can go on like this.

INTRODUCTION

ARE YOU BEING SQUEEZED BY YOUR MONEY?

"If you want to know your past life, look into your present condition; If you want to know your future, look into your present action."

—Padmisabba

"The future is a blank slate, so fill it with good stuff!"

—Patricia Stallworth

Everyday, all over the world, people are being *squeezed* by their money. You hear their stories everywhere. They're being *squeezed* by past money decisions; they're being *squeezed* by current bills that are taking over their lives; and they are being *squeezed* by a lack of savings that makes it nearly impossible for them to move forward and achieve any of the goals they really want. You might think these stories are limited to a select group of people, but shockingly, these stories occur in every age, income, and even education bracket—everyone is vulnerable!

10 Sure Signs You're Being Squeezed By Your Money

What does it feel like to be *squeezed* by your money? Sometimes we live with things one way for so long that it seems normal, and we can't imagine it any other way. But if you're being squeezed by your money, there's a problem, and usually you can do something about. Here are 10 sure signs you're being squeeze by your money. Check off any signs that apply to you...

- ❏ *Living paycheck to paycheck.* This is an extreme sign because just one missed paycheck could send you into a downward spiral. And, in most cases, it doesn't have to be that way. You can often break this cycle with minimal planning.
- ❏ *Thinking that credit lines and limits are a part of your income.* If every time you want to purchase something, the first thing that comes to mind is "Do I have enough room on my card and how much will this add to my monthly payment?" then you are confusing your money with someone else's. Remember, credit of any type is a loan, not part of your income.
- ❏ *You look forward to getting a large tax refund to have fun or get some of the things you want.* A large tax refund usually means you had too much money withheld from your paycheck and that you basically gave Uncle Sam an interest free loan for a year. It's not money the government is giving you, it's really a return of your hard earned money.
- ❏ *You avoid opening your bank and credit card statements because you don't really want to know how bad the situation is.* This is the same type of thinking that keeps people who might be sick from going to the doctor, but it doesn't help you in the long run. You have to know where you stand if you're ever going to make it better. So go ahead and look. You might be pleasantly surprised.

- ❑ *Despite the fact that you have a good income, you don't have any savings.* If savings is the last thing on your list there might not be anything left over to save so pay yourself first. Remember, it's not what you earn but what you keep that allows you to get ahead.

- ❑ *You don't know how much you really owe.* Not adding it up won't make it go away and that knowledge could help you make better decisions in the future. So add it all up and if you think it's too much make a plan to get out.

- ❑ *You're in a job, relationship, or location you don't like and you can't leave because you can't afford to.* I know this is real because I have been there. It's a miserable, stuck feeling that can cause you to settle for things instead of going after what you want. Always keep a personal stash of cash so you can live life on your terms.

- ❑ *Spending 50 percent or more of your income on housing.* Stretching to have more house than you can afford can have disastrous consequences. And it's just a house — it's not you. There are so many other things available to squeeze you, don't make it so easy for your money to be one of them.

- ❑ *You don't have an emergency fund to pay for unexpected expenses like car repairs so you have to use credit.* Having an emergency fund helps you stay healthy financially regardless of what life throws at you so determine an amount that you think will cover the average emergency and keep that amount on hand.

- ❑ *You don't have a financial plan for your future.* Knowing where you want to go and having a plan to get there is key to *squeezing* back. It doesn't have to be fancy but you do need the basics to help guide your decisions.

FOUR COMMON OBSTACLES THAT CAN KEEP YOU IN A 'SQUEEZE VICTIM' ROLE

Money is such a big part of our lives and we've built up so many emotions, and elaborate mechanisms around it that it's sometimes hard to determine when you are really a victim. As a result, you may end up making things more difficult on yourself than they have to be. So be on the lookout, you may be a squeeze victim if...

- **You have limiting attitudes or destructive behaviors related to money**. You learned most of your attitudes and behaviors about money from your parents, teachers, relatives, friends, the media, etc. at a very early age and if nothing has caused you to change them, they may be causing you to make money decisions on a subconscious level regardless of evidence to the contrary. For example, if your parents often fought about money, you may associate money with conflict and want to get rid of it as quickly as possible even when you have a savings goal.
- **You didn't have any formal financial education**. If you didn't get this type of information in school or at home, and you haven't spent much time since working on your money education, you may be missing out on important steps you could take to avoid being a victim.
- **You're suffering from information overload**. There is so much information about managing your money in the media and on the Internet that it's difficult to know what is right or who to believe. This can lead to analysis paralysis and no action on your part, and that is never good. Some action usually trumps no action.

- **You don't have a plan.** If you tend to make decisions on the fly with no real plan or sense of the impact of your actions on your future, you could end up just spinning your wheels and never really getting anywhere.

WHY *SQUEEZE* BACK NOW?

There's a saying, If not now, when? Every day you waste getting *squeezed* by your money means less time to build the financial future you want. Stop and imagine what your life could be like if you were the one doing the squeezing. And then develop a plan to *SQUEEZE* BACK!

The sooner you start the better, and this is critical when it comes to building wealth. *(See the chart below.)*

The Benefits of Investing Early and Often

	Kathy	Kelly	Kevin
Age:	25	35	45
Each person invests $100/mo until age 65 for a total of:	$48,000	$36,000	$24,000
With an 8 percent return at age 65 their accounts total:	$483,668	$215,635	$91,484

Even though Kathy only invested $12,000 more than Kelly and $24,000 more than Kevin, she ended up with $268,033 more than Kelly and $392,184 more than Kevin at age 65. Time and compounding or earning interest on your interest are the main reasons why Kathy was able to accumulate so much more money than Kelly and Kevin. The earlier you start the better.

The *Squeeze* System Solution

The number one secret about money that many people fail to understand is that money is just not that good at managing itself. And the common thread that runs through the majority of the *squeeze* stories I hear is the lack of a money management plan or system.

> THE #1 SECRET ABOUT MONEY THAT MANY PEOPLE FAIL TO UNDERSTAND IS THAT MONEY IS JUST NOT GOOD AT MANAGING ITSELF.

After years of working with clients at all levels, I noticed a troubling pattern. Many of my clients weren't really managing their money. They were just earning it and then hoping/praying/assuming/thinking that it would somehow magically manage itself. But that just doesn't work. So I designed the *Squeeze Your Money System* to provide them with an alternative to what I call MBC (Management By Chance). Unlike MBC, the *Squeeze Your Money System* provides a financial roadmap to follow to achieve your goals, to get out and stay out of debt, or to have money left over after paying your bills to do some of the things you really want to do because it keeps you in control of your money—not the other way around.

WHAT YOU'LL GET OUT OF SQUEEZE

Squeeze is based on twelve basic principles that I have sprinkled throughout the text *(see p. vii for a complete listing)*. They are really nothing more than common sense, however, in battles between our emotions and common sense; common sense is often the loser. That's why the *Squeeze* system is so important. It's an objective guide you can follow, so there's less chance for your emotions to take over. *Squeeze* was written specifically for everyday people —for people who want to get off the emotional roller coaster they are on because they never learned the basics of money management—for people who are tired of being *squeezed* by their money—for people who haven't yet developed a system to organize and manage their money—and for people who have gotten caught up in all that's going on today and basically lost their way when it comes to managing their money.

It's a book about getting back to basics and managing your money from the ground up so you can *squeeze* the most out of every dollar you have. And it's a "working" book. It's a combination text and workbook so you not only learn the steps to organize and manage your financial life, but you can add your information and immediately apply the system to your personal finances. And if you have computer access, you can download the templates from the *Squeeze* website (www.squeezeyourmoney.com) and work directly on your computer. However, I want to encourage you to complete the exercises by hand for at least the first three months so you can become intimately aware of your numbers. It's understanding your numbers that provides you with the knowledge to know when something is off or wrong so you can stop and say, Hey, wait a minute, and make changes, if necessary, to direct your money to the places you want it to go. Basically, the

Squeeze Your Money System prepares you to take over the job as the boss of your money. But I'm not going to kid you. There's also another side to *squeezing* back—it's called reality. While you may be able to have everything you want, you may not be able to have it all at the same time. This means prioritizing your *needs* and *wants*, possibly waiting longer to get some things, and even sacrificing in some areas to get the things you really want in others. But if you really want to take control, *Squeeze* is here for you.

WHO STANDS TO BENEFIT THE MOST FROM *SQUEEZE*?

While *Squeeze* will work for most people, it is especially helpful for people who...

- Are take-charge types who want to be in control of their finances and want to manage the process themselves.
- Want to work with their spouse or partner to manage their money better together.
- Have recently experienced an event that made their finances more complicated, such as marriage, a new job, a divorce, a new baby, or they received a lump sum of money like an inheritance or a settlement.
- Have had their finances managed by someone else in the past and now want or need to take over the job themselves.
- Have financial management problems, such as late charges and bounced checks that can be improved with organization.

HOW *SQUEEZE* IS ORGANIZED

Squeeze is divided into three parts. Each part is designed to assist you in building a system that will grow with you.

- **Part I: The *Squeeze Your Money System*.** Part I provides an overview of the *Squeeze Your Money System* and helps you ease into the *Squeeze Your Money* mindset.
- **Part II: The *Squeeze Your Money* Spending Plan.** Part II guides you through setting up a basic *Squeeze Spending Plan* to organize and keep your dollars on track.
- **Part III: *Squeeze Your Money* Action Strategies**. Part III applies the data from your *Squeeze Spending Plan* to manage other aspects of your personal finances—from developing a long-term plan for your future to attacking debt and managing your credit score.

SPECIAL ELEMENTS AND ICONS

Throughout this book, you'll find a variety of special elements—squeeze stories, sidebars, icons and other extras designed to call attention to special items of interest. In addition, each chapter ends with *Squeeze* Info Blocks that summarize the key points of the chapter and *Squeeze Action Items*—a list of exercises to either to follow up on the material in the current chapter or in preparation for the next one.

You can also find many of the worksheets and templates in this book on the *Squeeze Your Money* website as well as lots of additional information to help you stay on track on the *Squeeze* blog so visit often and leave us your comments.

www.squeezeyourmoney.com

FEATURED ICONS

Harvey serves as your advocate by asking questions to clarify parts of the *Squeeze Your Money System*

Harriet offers bright ideas and key tips and strategies to make your system run more smoothly

Squeeze Points summarize the key elements in the chapter

Squeeze Action Items —Exercises to fill in the blanks and practice your skills

RESOURCES & TERMS —These are included at the end of each chapter or major section

Squeeze Stories and updates

Join us! Become a part of the *Squeeze* Community. Send us your *squeeze* story, questions, or comments to:

info@squeezeyourmoney.com

PART 1

CHAPTER ONE

SQUEEZE YOUR MONEY!

"If a man has money, it is usually a sign, too, that he knows how to take care of it; don't imagine his money is easy to get simply because he has plenty of it."
—Edgar Watson Howe

Squeeze Principle #1: Money is just not good at managing itself, so don't let it. Take control, and make it work for you!

Left to its own devices money will slip through your fingers, burn a hole in your pocket, and make a mess of your financial life. It needs input from you to achieve its highest potential, which is to go to work for you.

LEFT TO ITS OWN DEVICES MONEY WILL SLIP THROUGH YOUR FINGERS, BURN A HOLE IN YOUR POCKET, AND MAKE A MESS OF YOUR FINANCES.

The *Squeeze Your Money System* was developed to give you the strategies and tools to take over the job of managing your money. It's simple, it's easy to follow and it doesn't take a lot of time to complete, typically less than three hours a month. So it's time to stop hiding behind whatever is stopping you. It's time to put your money to work for you. It's time to SQUEEZE YOUR MONEY!

How *Squeeze* Works

The choices you make with your money has a direct impact on what you can do and how far you can go. And to make the best choices, you need good information. The *Squeeze Your Money System (SYMS)* was designed to provide you with the information and tools you need to make better choices regarding how you use and spend your money.

As you go through *SYMS*, you will have an opportunity to see the results of your current money choices and to make conscious decisions about how you want to proceed going forward. This information will allow you to take control of your finances and your destiny by learning to make choices that get you closer to where you want to be. Remember, earning money is just the first part of the story. Putting it to work for you is the next part. And the best way to do that is with a comprehensive plan of action.

THE ELEMENTS OF *SQUEEZE*

The *Squeeze Your Money System (SYMS)* is a step-by-step program to organize and manage your financial life. It consists of two basic parts: the *Squeeze* Spending Plan (SSP) and *Squeeze* Action Strategies (SAS). Both parts of *SYMS* can be used separately, but when used in

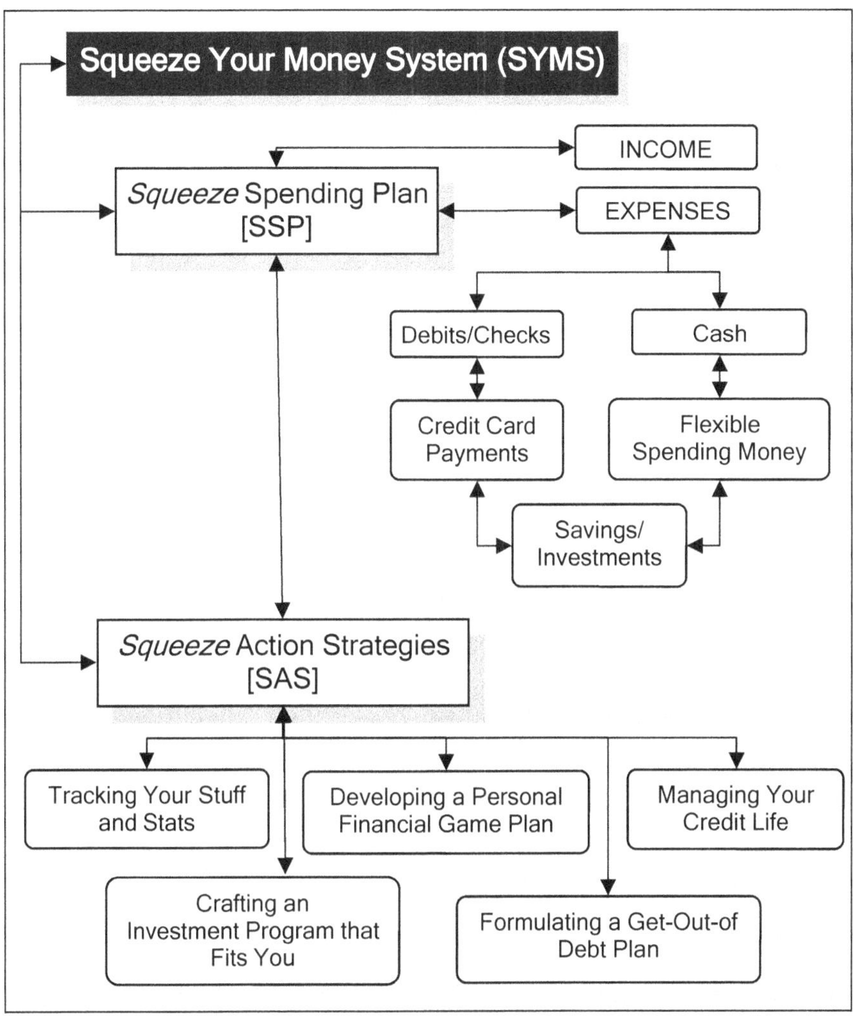

conjunction with each other, they form a continuous loop with each part having a direct impact on the other, just as your spending impacts the types of actions you can take and vice versa. *(See the diagram above.)*

1. ***The Squeeze Your Money Spending Plan (SSP)*** – SSP is the core component of *SYMS*. It brings together all of the elements that make up your income and expenses into a

workable spending plan that provides a financial road map. It helps you and your dollars stay on track, and it prevents you from straying too far off course with a form of checks and balances.

The main focus of SSP is on *how* you spend your money so you can control and/or limit the ways your money leaves you. SSP lays the foundation for all other parts of *SYMS*.

2. *Squeeze Your Money Action Strategies (SAS)* – SAS uses the data from your *Squeeze* Spending Plan to proactively manage all other aspects of your personal finances—from funding your goals to getting out of debt to managing your credit score. SAS focuses on the essential elements in five key areas:

   - Tracking your stuff and stats (the things you own and owe) so you always know where you are financially. *(Chapter 11)*
   - Developing a personal financial game plan to serve as a guide to get you where you want to go. *(Chapter 12)*
   - Crafting a personal investment program that fits you and your goals. *(Chapter 13)*
   - Managing your credit life to keep your records accurate and working for you. *(Chapter 14)*
   - Formulating a get-out and stay-out-of-debt plan so all your extra dollars go to places you want them to. *(Chapter 15)*

The essentials in these five areas provide a foundation to manage all the basic parts of your financial life. Then if you want more information in these or other areas of your personal finances, you can build on this foundation using other resources or another book in the *Squeeze Your Money* series.

Each step of the *SYMS* process builds on the previous one, and the system is designed to be completed in order, so skipping ahead, especially in SSP, is not recommended. Think of the process as more of a marathon than a sprint so take your time, complete each part, and be sure you understand how it works before you move on to the next one. As you personalize your system, if changes are necessary, make them gradually, as drastic changes could lead to more stress and eventually cause you to walk away from your plan. By completing *SYMS,* you are taking care of your money—an important element that impacts every part of your life. Once you complete your personalized system, you'll be well on your way to effectively managing your finances, maximizing your dollars, and reducing your money stress.

Hey, wait a minute. What makes *Squeeze* different from other programs? Don't they all do the same thing?

Good question, Harvey. Actually they're not all the same. Most programs just focus either on a budget or general financial planning and investing. However, *Squeeze* is a complete system that includes both a detailed spending plan and the steps to follow after you develop your spending plan so you can use that information to manage all of the other elements of your financial life.

The *Squeeze Your Money* Mindset

There's an old saying, "If you think you can or you think you can't, you're right," and I think this is especially true when it comes to managing your finances. That's why I want to start by asking you to let go of any lingering fears, doubts, or self-recriminations you might have about your ability to take on this task. To get the most out of *SYMS,* you will need to commit to a *"Squeeze Your Money mindset,"* which is essentially a *"can do"* attitude. Once you do, you can begin creating your own solutions using the tools and strategies outlined here.

Let's face it—sometimes just the thought of managing your money can make you want to run in the opposite direction. And while managing your money is not the easiest thing you'll ever do, it's not the toughest thing either. It's very doable, but it will be so much easier if you're not holding on to past fears, failures, or doubts. Completing *SYMS* can literally change your life.

One element that makes this task so difficult is the fact that money, despite its importance to us, is in many ways an abstract concept that can sometimes be difficult to wrap your head around. After all, our paychecks are direct deposited, we pay bills by check or online, and now we can even charge fast food, so we rarely have to touch real money and that makes the task of trying to manage it even more mind-boggling. With this in mind, one of your first tasks in *squeezing your money* will be to bring your money back into the realm of reality so you can touch it and get a clear picture of what's coming in, what's going out, and where it's all going to help you determine what is and what isn't working for you.

How you manage your money has such a great impact on every aspect of your life, and the sooner you get started the sooner you can begin to see results. So gather up your best can do attitude and let's get started!

But FIRST, if you will be working with a spouse or partner, read *Squeeze for Couples* below.

SQUEEZE FOR COUPLES

Since it's highly unlikely that you and your significant other will agree on everything, if you share one or more bank accounts, you will have a better chance of succeeding with the *Squeeze Your Money System* if you put some ground rules in place from the start.

Here are five important ground rules to discuss with your partner:

1. **Determine who will take the lead in managing the system.** While you should both participate in setting up the system, once it's up and running, the ongoing monthly maintenance can easily be performed by one person. Some couples elect to have one partner take the lead, while others prefer to share this task by switching off every six months so they both understand what it takes to keep the system going.
2. **Agree that being the lead manager doesn't make you the boss of the other.** If managing the system is your job, it doesn't make you superior to your partner, so when you give your partner an update, don't turn it into a lecture. And if your partner makes errors, such as

Continued on the next page

forgetting to tell you about a purchase or an ATM withdrawal he or she spent more than the amount allocated, talk with him or her about it and also point out any errors you made as well. You job is to summarize account activity, not to assign blame.

Remember, you are partners and you both have an equal say.

3. **Agree that one of the responsibilities of the lead manager is to communicate fully with the other partner.** Aside from the responsibility to manage the accounts accurately, you are also responsible for keeping your partner fully informed. It's not fair to use your partner's distance from the details against her or him. Don't hide transactions and don't use your role as an opportunity to make financial decisions you know he or she would not agree to.

4. **Agree that if the system needs changes, you will make the changes together.** The only constant in life is change, and every system will need to evolve to accommodate life's changes. If you find that one component is not working for one of you or if something needs adjusting, you must both be willing to work toward a resolution. Commit to keep your plan and then work to make it work for you.

5. **Commit to follow the plan.** For any system to work, it must be followed completely and consistently. This means that both of you must do your part. Just as the partner who takes on the role of the lead manager must agree to communicate fully (#3), the other partner must also do his or her part. Don't make the lead

Continued on the next page

manager have to track you down for information and receipts. Don't pretend like you don't understand the system. (If you truly don't understand how things work, then both of you need to fill in the gaps so everyone is clear about how the system works.) And don't keep saying, "I forgot" or "But I needed it." If you don't give the lead manager the necessary information and cooperation, you'll make it impossible for the system to work.

Whether you and your spouse agree on most things or nothing at all, setting some ground rules at the beginning will greatly increase your chances of success.

SQUEEZE POINTS:

- ***Squeeze Principle #1: Money is just not good at managing itself, so don't let it. Take control and make it work for you!***

- The *Squeeze Your Money System* provides the strategies and tools to manage your money. It's composed of two basic parts: The *Squeeze* Spending Plan (SSP) that tracks *how* you spend your money so you can manage or limit the ways your money leaves you; and *Squeeze* Action Strategies (SAS) that use the information you collect in your spending plan to manage the other key areas of your financial life—from developing a personal financial roadmap to managing your credit life. Both parts are dependent on each other because the actions you take immediately impact your spending plan and that determines the types of actions you can take.

SQUEEZE POINTS *(continued):*

- Maintaining a *Squeeze Your Money mindset* or a "can do" attitude is essential as you go through the *Squeeze Your Money System (SYMS).* And if you will be working with a spouse or partner, it is important to set some ground rules from the start regarding how you will manage the system and the roles that each of you system and the roles that each of you will play.

SQUEEZE ACTION ITEMS:

1. Review and commit to a *Squeeze Your Money mindset,* and if you'll be working with a spouse or partner, develop a set of ground rules to work together.

SQUEEZE STORY UPDATE:

Stephanie and Ron

Ron and I have agreed to all of the suggestions in the *Squeeze for Couples.* In fact, we drew up a contract that we both signed. Then we decided we would share the responsibility for taking care of our money. We agreed that for the first three months we would do everything together (even the maintenance part of the system) and then switch off every six months after that so that both of us would always know what's going on and how to manage the system if the other was unavailable.

PART 2

CHAPTER TWO

THE *SQUEEZE* SPENDING PLAN

"Though no one can go back and make a brand new start, anyone can start from now and make a brand new ending."

– Author Unknown

How you spend your money has a direct impact on every area of your life so having a spending plan or a model to work from is a great way to ensure that you make choices that work for you. The *Squeeze* Spending Plan (SSP) is based on a simple business model—spend your money on paper first so you can plan where you want it to go. This puts you in control and gives you the opportunity to *squeeze* the most out of every dollar.

Elements of SSP

Your *Squeeze* Spending Plan (SSP) plays an important role because it lays the foundation for every other part of your life by providing essential information you can use to make informed decisions. It does this by bringing together all of the elements that make up your income and expenses so you have a roadmap to follow. The main focus of SSP is on *how* you spend your money. This allows you to control and/or limit the ways your money leaves you, and in many cases, just making small shifts in how you spend your money can produce really big results.

WHAT'S IN THE *SQUEEZE* SPENDING PLAN?

The *Squeeze* Spending Plan (SSP) is a roadmap for spending your dollars in any given month. It's a basic tool designed to work for all income levels and the one page summary format makes it easy to complete. Once you setup your plan, it usually only requires about three hours a month to keep it up and running. *(See the example on p. 24.)*

The *Squeeze* Spending Plan has two basic parts:

A. INCOME – this forms the foundation of your spending. The goal here is to spend less than you earn on needs and wants so you have money available to fund your savings and goals.

B. EXPENSES – expenses are broken into five basic categories:

   (1) DEBITS/CHECKS – this includes debit card payments and checks you write each month as well as online payments or authorized payments for recurring expenses.

   (2) CASH – this is used to cover ordinary weekly spending and this category needs no further tracking.

   (3) CREDIT CARD PAYMENTS – this consists of either

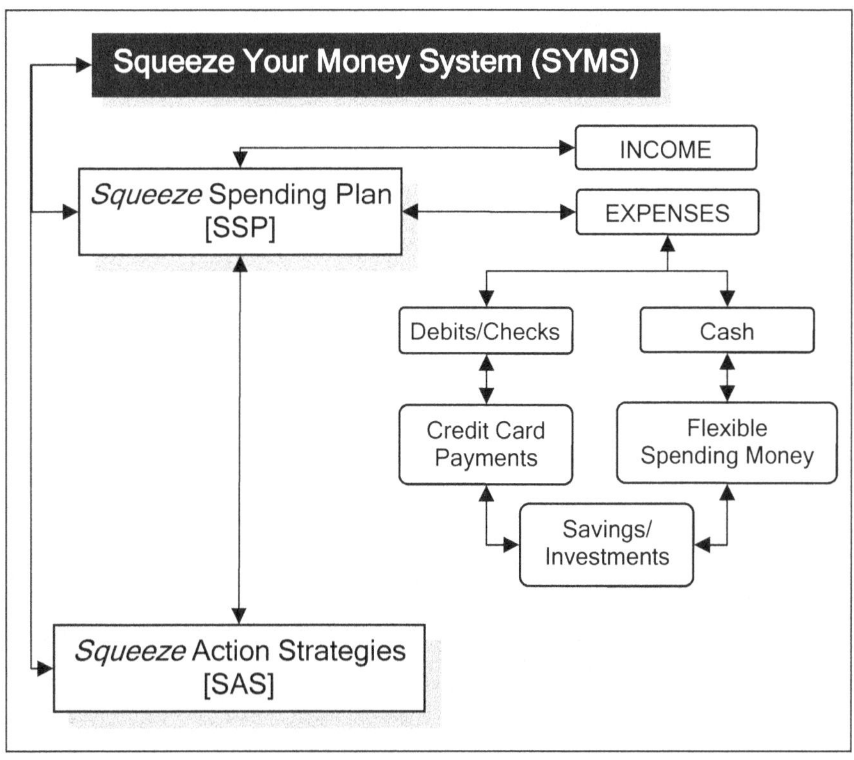

the minimum monthly payment or the amount you plan to pay for all of your cards combined.

(4) FLEXIBLE SPENDING MONEY— this covers spending in other areas that don't quite fit into any of the above categories.

(5) SAVINGS/INVESTMENTS – this includes dollars to fund an emergency fund and your goals.

In addition, each expense category has its own background worksheet that can be used to add as much detail as you like so you understand what all of the summary numbers are based on. Then the bottom line from each

SQUEEZE SPENDING PLAN (SSP) SUMMARY

Month/Yr. ____________ End Date ____________ Weeks ____________

INCOME	PLAN	ACTUAL	DIFFERENCE
Income *(Take-home pay)*			
Income *(Take-home pay)*			
Other Income			
LAST MONTH - Positive Bottom Line			
TOTAL INCOME			
EXPENSES	**PLAN**	**ACTUAL**	**DIFFERENCE**
LAST MONTH - Negative Bottom Line			
(1) DEBITS / CHECKS			
(2) CASH ________ x ____________ (# of weeks, dollars/wk)			
(3) CREDIT CARD PAYMENTS			
(4) FLEXIBLE SPENDING MONEY			
(5) SAVINGS / INVESTMENTS			
TOTAL EXPENSES			
BOTTOM LINE	**PLAN**	**ACTUAL**	**DIFFERENCE**
(Income minus Expenses)			

* Additional copies of all worksheets can be downloaded from www.squeezeyourmoney.com.

worksheet goes onto the main SSP page shown above in the appropriate category. We'll go over the SSP in more detail in the following chapters so you can get comfortable with how it all works. As we do, follow along and add your information to create a Master *Squeeze* Spending Plan template. The Master SSP you create can then serve as a guide to complete your spending plan each month.

STEPS TO BUILD A *SQUEEZE* SPENDING PLAN BASED ON YOUR LIFESTYLE

The basic function of SSP is to collect, organize, and track your income and expenses so you can maximize your dollars. And it's basically a four-step process:

Step 1: Calculate your total monthly income.

Step 2: Compile a list of your monthly expenses in each of the five categories.

Step 3: Subtract your total monthly expenses from your total monthly income to get a bottom line.

Step 4: Review your bottom line and if the difference is positive, decide what you want to do with the extra money. Or, if it's negative, keep working on it until the bottom line is zero or positive.

And *voila!* A *Squeeze* Spending Plan is born.

Once your plan is up and running, you will need to work on it for only a short time each month to keep it up to date. Monthly maintenance consists of verifying your account balances and recording your actual spending for the month just finished. The first two columns labeled PLAN and ACTUAL are for those numbers. The third column, DIFFERENCE, highlights the categories in which your *actual* spending differed from what you *planned* so you can make corrections in the coming months. Then you're ready to prepare a new SSP form for the coming month and pay your bills.

While it's okay to use estimates in creating your Master SSP form, when you work on your Monthly SSP, use the exact amounts because they should be available. The main purpose of creating a Master SSP is to have a guide to follow in creating your monthly spending plans, and to get an overview of your current financial situation—to see if it's okay, if it needs a minor tune-up, or if it needs a major overhaul. Finally, going through this process each month allows you to become familiar with your numbers—to see their impact on your bottom line. And if you decide to make changes, you have all the information you need.

Hey, wait a minute. Why should I go through all of this work when I can just use my bank's program online?

Good question, Harvey. But you should know that while there are some good online resources available, many are focused on taking a look after the fact and not on real planning like *Squeeze.* Also, I recommend that you do at least the first three months of your plan in pencil so you can get familiar with your numbers. This will give you the ability to recognize potential problems quickly. After that you can use *Squeeze* online or even another program. However, if you decide to use another program, be sure to come back and update your information with *Squeeze* at least once every six months so you always know where you are with your spending and overall financially.

WHAT MAKES *SQUEEZE* DIFFERENT?

Squeeze is different from other spending plans and budgets in two key ways. The first is in the level of detail and thoroughness of *Squeeze*. Most books devote only a few pages to developing a spending plan or budget and so much is left out, especially about how to implement a plan and maintain it. *Squeeze,* on the other hand, is all about the details because if you don't understand the details it's easy to get off track, and you can't begin to make changes for the better or fix things if you're not sure what you're doing or why. The good news is, once you understand your situation better, you can skip a lot of the detail and only revisit it once or twice a year to be sure you stay on track.

> SQUEEZE IS ALL ABOUT BECOMING AWARE OF THE DETAILS THAT MAKE UP YOUR FINANCIAL LIFE BECAUSE IF YOU DON'T UNDERSTAND THE DETAILS, YOU WON'T KNOW WHEN SOMETHING IS WRONG, WHAT TO DO TO FIX IT, OR HOW TO SQUEEZE THE MOST OUT OF IT.

Second, because of the *Squeeze* Action Strategies, you can put the information from your spending plan to work immediately. You can make informed decisions about managing the rest of your financial life and you can see how the spending decisions you make impact your actions and vice versa. Then you can make changes to get the outcome you want and see the results quickly.

Revisiting the *Squeeze Your Money* Mindset

The *Squeeze* Spending Plan (SSP) helps you organize and manage your money. In order for it to work, though, you have to use it on a monthly basis – even when you get off track and overspend. In fact if you get off track, all you have to do is calculate the amount you overspent and carry the corrections into the next month's spending plan. *(Note: This is an example of the checks and balances to keep you from straying too far off course.) Squeeze* is a very flexible tool and the goal is to keep you moving toward achieving the things that mean the most to you.

However, even with the best of intentions, it's not unusual for doubts or uncertainties to crop up as you go through the *Squeeze Your Money System* so before this happens I want to go back to the *"can do"* attitude we talked about earlier and address four common thoughts that can trip you up:

1. *Believing that if you create a Squeeze Spending Plan you won't have as much money to spend as you used to, or want to.*

   Antidote: Remember, you can't change the quantity of the money you have simply by writing it down. And you won't have less by knowing what you have and planning where you want it to go.

2. *Thinking you don't make enough to even bother.*

Antidote: Whether you have a lot or a little, you will benefit from organizing and planning your spending. The less money you have, the more important it is to get the best use of each dollar. If one of your goals is to attract more money in your life, you must first take care of and responsibility for what you have now. Once you do, you'll be better prepared to appreciate and enjoy greater wealth as it comes into your life.

3. *Believing that the Squeeze Spending Plan will take away your freedom to spend spontaneously without feeling guilty.*

   Antidote: Your *Squeeze* Spending Plan includes "fun or flexible money" you can spend any way you like. And because it's in the plan, you can make spontaneous purchases without feeling guilty or jeopardizing other necessary expenses or goals.

4. *Thinking that it's better not to know your true financial situation. In other words, believing that ignorance is bliss.*

   Antidote: This same type of thinking keeps some people from going to the doctor when they think they may be ill because they don't want to know how bad the situation could be. But burying your head in the sand is never the answer. Learning to manage your money now is not only good for your present, but it's invaluable for your future. And, like most things, the longer you put it off, the more missed opportunities you will have, and the tougher the process is likely to be.

So get started, and don't let doubts slow you down.

SQUEEZE POINTS:

- The *Squeeze* Spending Plan (SSP) consists of two basic components—income and expenses. Your expenses are broken down further into five categories: debits/ checks, cash, credit card payments, flexible spending money, and savings/investments.
- Creating a monthly spending plan is a four-step process: (1) Calculate your total income; (2) Add up all of your expenses; (3) Subtract your expenses from your income; (4) Review your bottom line. If it's positive decide how to spend the extra money. Or if it's negative, keeping working on it until the bottom line is zero or positive.
- *Squeeze* is different from other spending plans or budgets in the level of detail it provides on how to build and maintain a spending plan as well as allowing you to use the information you compile immediately with the *Squeeze* Action Strategies in Part III.
- Revisit the *Squeeze Your Money* mindset as often as you need to stay on track. Avoid falling into some common traps, like thinking that creating a spending plan will somehow limit the amount of money you have available to spend.

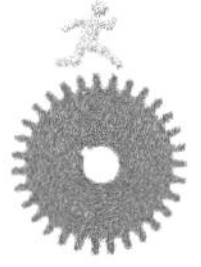

SQUEEZE ACTION ITEMS:

1. Make 15 copies of the blank *Squeeze* Spending Summary spreadsheet. ***Note:*** *Full-size copies can be downloaded from www.squeezeyourmoney.com.*

2. Purchase or have the following items available:

   - ❑ a three-ring binder to keep your spending plans and notes organized
   - ❑ dividers or tabs (one for each month), and one for your Master SSP
   - ❑ a calculator
   - ❑ pencils

   *Plan to complete your first two to three monthly SSP's by hand in pencil. Then once you are comfortable with the process, you can work in pen or online.

Note: *Squeeze Your Money Kits are available on our website. The kits include all of the materials you need to get your plan up and running, including a binder, labeled dividers, worksheets, checklists, a debit register, pencils, and a calculator.*

Visit www.squeezeyourmoney.com/store for more information.

SQUEEZE STORY:

Kirstin

I have always equated managing money right up there with going to the dentist—something I know I should do at least once in a while but something to be avoided as long as possible, though I have made several attempts. I started a 401(k) at a previous employer, but I never signed the final paper to start funding it, and there was a 5 percent match. I know money down the drain. I set up an IRA and had the best of intentions to put something in it, but I haven't done that either. I even started a budget, but I didn't know what to do with it. I always thought that Mr. Right would come along and handle all of this kind of stuff, but he hasn't shown up yet, and the clock is ticking. I'm still young (41), but I would like to retire someday, whether I meet Mr. Right or not.

The problem is I've waited so long I'm scared to do anything. I'm not sure where to start and what to do first, and I'm terrified that I will make a mistake, and I don't think I can afford to make too many of those.

CHAPTER THREE

CALCULATING YOUR REAL INCOME

"Money isn't the most important thing in life, but it's reasonably close to oxygen on the 'gotta have it' scale."
—Zig Ziglar

Squeeze Principle #2: Throwing more money at problems isn't always the answer. Squeeze your money first. Then look to other options!

To get a sense of the reasoning behind *Principle* #2, think back to when you first started working. How much money were you earning then, and how much are you earning now? Chances are if you've worked for awhile, you're earning more money now. So are you better off now? Do you have more money in savings? Do you have less debt? If you answered no to any of these questions, you understand the reasoning behind the principle—more money does not always solve your problems. In fact, as you earn more money, the tendency is to increases your expenses as well. But if you were living okay with less money, wouldn't a more prudent strategy be to keep your expenses constant or allow for moderate changes and increase your savings as your income grows?

Calculating just how much money you have available to meet your expenses and fund your goals is the first step in the *Squeeze* Spending Plan (SSP). Understanding what you have available each month allows you to *squeeze* the most out of every dollar without overspending. While this sounds like a simple task, depending on how you get paid, you may be actually shortchanging or overextending yourself without even realizing it.

How Much Money Do You Really Have to Spend?

Have you ever noticed that there are more weeks in a year than fit neatly into 12 months? Fifty-two weeks just doesn't fit neatly into 12 four-week months. And this difference can sometimes cause you to make a mistake in calculating your monthly income, especially if you are paid weekly or biweekly. If your take-home pay is $500 a week, you might, for example, jump to the conclusion that your monthly take-home pay is $2,000. However, net pay of $500 a week doesn't equal $2,000 a month, because there are a few times during the year when you get a fifth paycheck. And here's the proof:

$500 per week × 52 weeks = $26,000 annual net pay
$2,000 per month × 12 months = $24,000 annual net pay

Making this kind of mistake would cause you to shortchange the amount you have available to spend by $2,000 a year, or $167 a month!

PLANNING FOR EXTRA INCOME OR EXPENSES

If you're paid weekly or biweekly, approximately once quarter you could receive an extra paycheck. And if you know it's coming, you can plan for it and include it in your spending plan. On the other hand, if you are paid monthly or semi-monthly, every once in a while your expenses will be greater than usual. One of the main reasons that traditional budgets often fail is because they don't allow for extra income or expenses that normally occur over time. When these events occur everything gets thrown out of balance – you could end up with more expenses and not enough income to cover them or you might believe you have extra income and use it unwisely.

> ONE OF THE MAIN REASONS THAT TRADITIONAL BUDGETS FAIL IS THAT THEY DON'T ALLOW FOR EXTRA INCOME OR EXPENSES THAT NORMALLY OCCUR OVER TIME.

One of the best ways to see this visually is to take a current calendar and highlight all of your pay days. When you do this you should see a pattern emerge of four-week months and five-week months so you can see at a glance when you will receive an extra paycheck or possibly have extra expenses . (See the example on the next page.) Once you create a calendar with your specific pay days circled, be sure to keep a copy in your binder so you can refer to it each month to determine if a 4-week or a 5-week month is coming up so you can plan appropriately.

2012 Calendar with weekly Friday pay days

2012

January

S	M	T	W	T	F	S
1	2	3	4	5	**6**	7
8	9	10	11	12	**13**	14
15	16	17	18	19	**20**	21
22	23	24	25	26	**27**	28
29	30	31				

February

S	M	T	W	T	F	S
			1	2	**3**	4
5	6	7	8	9	**10**	11
12	13	14	15	16	**17**	18
19	20	21	22	23	**24**	25
26	27	28	29			

March

S	M	T	W	T	F	S
				1	**2**	3
4	5	6	7	8	**9**	10
11	12	13	14	15	**16**	17
18	19	20	21	22	**23**	24
25	26	27	28	29	**30**	31

April

S	M	T	W	T	F	S
1	2	3	4	5	**6**	7
8	9	10	11	12	**13**	14
15	16	17	18	19	**20**	21
22	23	24	25	26	**27**	28
29	30					

May

S	M	T	W	T	F	S
		1	2	3	**4**	5
6	7	8	9	10	**11**	12
13	14	15	16	17	**18**	19
20	21	22	23	24	**25**	26
27	28	29	30	31		

June

S	M	T	W	T	F	S
					1	2
3	4	5	6	7	**8**	9
10	11	12	13	14	**15**	16
17	18	19	20	21	**22**	23
24	25	26	27	28	**29**	30

July

S	M	T	W	T	F	S
1	2	3	4	5	**6**	7
8	9	10	11	12	**13**	14
15	16	17	18	19	**20**	21
22	23	24	25	26	**27**	28
29	30	31				

August

S	M	T	W	T	F	S
			1	2	**3**	4
5	6	7	8	9	**10**	11
12	13	14	15	16	**17**	18
19	20	21	22	23	**24**	25
26	27	28	29	30	**31**	

September

S	M	T	W	T	F	S
						1
2	3	4	5	6	**7**	8
9	10	11	12	13	**14**	15
16	17	18	19	20	**21**	22
23	24	25	26	27	**28**	29
30						

October

S	M	T	W	T	F	S
	1	2	3	4	**5**	6
7	8	9	10	11	**12**	13
14	15	16	17	18	**19**	20
21	22	23	24	25	**26**	27
28	29	30	31			

November

S	M	T	W	T	F	S
				1	**2**	3
4	5	6	7	8	**9**	10
11	12	13	14	15	**16**	17
18	19	20	21	22	**23**	24
25	26	27	28	29	**30**	

December

S	M	T	W	T	F	S
						1
2	3	4	5	6	**7**	8
9	10	11	12	13	**14**	15
16	17	18	19	20	**21**	22
23	24	25	26	27	**28**	29
30	31					

CALCULATING YOUR SPENDING MONEY

Using a copy of your paystub(s), complete an *Income Deductions Worksheet* on the next page for each job you (or your spouse) have. Be sure to include all of your deductions, including taxes, retirement plan contributions, and medical deductions. When you finish, place a copy in your binder as a reminder of the expenses you are already covering, so you don't double count them in the following chapters. Unless there are major changes throughout the year, you will only need to update this worksheet once a year.

Next, calculate the amount of money you have available to spend each month by completing the *Monthly Income Worksheet* on p. 39. Fill in the name of the income source and your take-home pay for each job in the Monthly Plan column of the worksheet.

If you receive commissions or other income that fluctuates from month to month, estimate the monthly total that you can reasonably expect to receive and include that amount on the *Monthly Income Worksheet* as well. Leave out small, occasional income that you can't rely on. However, be sure to include all steady and reliable income such as child support payments or alimony. It's okay to use estimates in completing your Master SSP, however plan to use the actual numbers when completing your monthly SSP.

Squeeze: Income Deductions Worksheet

Instructions: Using your paystub, list all of the deductions and calculate your net income or take-home pay for each pay period. Complete a separate form for each job that has deductions.

1.	Gross Income per pay period	$ ______________
	Minus:	
	Taxes	
	Federal	$ ______________
	State	$ ______________
	Local/City	$ ______________
	Social Security (FICA)	$ ______________
	Medicare	$ ______________
2.	Total taxes withheld	$ ______________
	Automatic Payroll Deductions	
	Health Insurance	$ ______________
	Life Insurance	$ ______________
	Disability Insurance	$ ______________
	Dental Insurance	$ ______________
	Charitable Contributions	$ ______________
	Retirement Plan 401(k)/403(b), etc	$ ______________
	Retirement Plan Loan Repayment	$ ______________
	Deferred Compensation Plan	$ ______________
	Employee Stock Purchase Plan	$ ______________
	Flexible Spending Acct/FSA/Section 125	$ ______________
	Other Automatic Drafts for Investments	$ ______________
	Other Automatic Drafts for Expenses	$ ______________
3.	Total payroll deductions	$ ______________
4.	Net Income per pay period	$ ______________
	(Line 1 - [Line 2 + Line 3])	

Squeeze: Monthly Income Worksheet

Instructions: List all of your income (take-home pay only) for the month. Be sure to include every type of income you can count on, including tips, commissions, alimony, and child support.

SOURCE OF INCOME	Weeks 1-2	Weeks 3-4	Week #5	MONTHLY PLAN	MONTHLY ACTUAL	DIFFERENCE
TOTAL						

* Additional blank copies of the Income Deductions Worksheet and the Monthly Income Worksheet are located at www.squeezeyourmoney.com.

Hey, wait a minute. What if my pay varies from month to month? What number should I put in? I own my own business and some months are better (or worse) than others.

Good question, Harvey. A fluctuating or unpredictable income can pose some special issues and require adjustments in calculating the amount of money you have available to spend each month. If you own your own business or if you receive most of your income from commissions or other sources that can vary from month to month, read the sidebar on the next page for options you can use to calculate your monthly income for SSP.

Including Unpredictable Income in Your *Squeeze* Spending Plan

So far we have been going on the assumption that the amount of your income is relatively constant and predictable. But what if it's not? If you receive commissions, tips or income from other sources that fluctuates or is unpredictable and it is your main source of income, then you may need to make some adjustments in how you calculate your monthly income.

There are two basic methods you can use to calculate fluctuating or unpredictable income for your SSP:

- **The Variable-Spending Method** —This method allows your level of spending to move up and down with changes in your income.
- **The Fixed-Spending Method** — This method keeps your level of spending constant regardless of the ups and downs in your income.

In each case, having a "cash cushion" of at least one month's expenses is critical. A cash cushion is a stash of cash you keep in a savings or other account. Having one gives you the freedom to pay your expenses on a set schedule regardless of when your paycheck arrives and to stay on track if you experience a shortfall one month. Basically, the money in your cash cushion sits in your account and you can dip into it as needed to pay your expenses. Then as your paychecks are deposited, your cash cushion gets replenished. In other words, it never leaves. It just gets used and rebuilt month after month.

Continued on the next page

The Variable-Spending Method

With the Variable-Spending method, you use the amount of money received in the preceding month as your income for the current month. There's no guesswork because you don't spend it until you have it. This method is totally dependent on having a cash cushion of at least one month's expenses to get started.

The Fixed-Spending Method

The Fixed-Spending method keeps your level of spending constant regardless of the ups and downs in your income and is best used by people who have been in a job long enough to have a realistic sense of how much income they can expect on a monthly basis.

To use the Fixed-Spending method, estimate a reasonable amount of income for a typical month being careful not to overestimate this figure. It's better to start with a conservative number and end with a happy surprise at the end of the month than to end up in the red. Once you have a realistic number, stick with it for three months. Then check your estimate by calculating an average income based on the actual amount you received. If you consistently brought in more than your estimate and want to increase the income amount in SSP, do so gradually. On the other hand, if you have constantly fallen short, consider scaling back on your income projections and your expenses to see if you can get your expenses in line with your actual income.

However, if the actual amount is right in line with your estimate, congratulate yourself and continue using the

Continued on the next page

same estimate over the next three months. Then calculate your average income again. When you are comfortable with this method, you may want to check your estimates less often, like every six months.

The Fixed-Spending method is riskier than the Variable method since you are spending money you may not earn. You can reduce the risk by estimating an income amount lower than you expect. Then any positive differences can accumulate as savings.

Which Method Is Best for You?

Neither one is better than the other, so pick the one that best fits your style of living and spending. Some people find they want to count on a fixed spending amount; changing their spending each month to accommodate changes in their income doesn't appeal to them. They are confident they will earn enough money to support their own spending level so they select the Fixed-Spending method. While others want the ability to live free from the risk of ever going in the red and to splurge after achieving a really big month. They select the Variable-Spending method. Pick one, or try both, then stick with the one that works best for you.

CASE STUDY: The Variable-Spending Method

Harvey is a business owner who experiences fluctuations in his income from month to month. The chart below shows the income he received and how he reported it on SSP using the Variable-Spending method. In each case, he received the money before he counted it as income for the next month. Since he is not sure how much he will receive each month, using the Variable method keeps him from spending more than he earns.

Harvey's Monthly Income	Income Listed on Harvey's SSP
January - Harvey has $3,000 in a Cash Cushion that he expects will last one month. He spends this in the first month while receiving income from his business of $2,700.	$3,000
February - Since he already has $2,700 in the bank, he uses this amount as his new income figure and he has to cut back on some of his expenses. During this month he earns $2,900 from his business.	$2,700
March - This month Harvey spends the $2,900 he earned last month and a new ad campaign increases his earnings to $3,500 this month.	$2,900
April - What amount will Harvey list on his SSP?	$______

ADDING INCOME TO YOUR MASTER SSP

Once you complete the *Monthly Income Worksheet,* total your income and place that total in the INCOME section of your Master SSP Summary worksheet in the PLAN column. *(See Harvey's Summary SSP on p. 46)*

SQUEEZE POINTS:

- ***Squeeze Principle #2: Throwing more money at problems isn't always the answer. Squeeze your money first. Then look to other options!***
- One of the main reasons that people overspend is that they don't know exactly how much money they have to spend. If you get paid weekly or biweekly, you can expect an extra paycheck every once in a while. And if you get paid monthly or semi-monthly, you will need to stretch your income about once a quarter to accommodate a more expenses.
- If you have fluctuating or unpredictable income, you may need to make some adjustments. Two methods that you can use to calculate your monthly income are the Fixed and the Variable method. There are pros and cons to both methods and you should choose one based on your style and spending habits.

SQUEEZE ACTION ITEMS:

1. Take a current annual calendar and circle all of your pay days. This will allow you to see when additional paychecks or additional expenses will be coming. Place a copy in your binder.
2. Label one copy of the Summary SSP form 'MASTER' and fill in the End Date and the number of weeks for the coming month at the top of the page.
3. Complete the *Income Deductions Worksheet* and then calculate your monthly income using the *Monthly Income Worksheet*. Be sure to include your net or take-home pay and any additional income sources such as tips, commissions, or bonuses. Total your income and put the total in the INCOME section of your MASTER SSP Summary form in the PLAN column.

SQUEEZE STORY:

John and Carol

Carol and I had a really rough year last year. I got downsized, and our portfolio took a big hit, so in many ways, it almost feels like we are starting over, but we don't want to make the same mistakes. This time we want to take control of our money so we don't end up in the same fix if this happens again...like having to take money out of our retirement plans to buy groceries.

[1] Blank copies are available at www.squeezeyourmoney.com.

Harvey's Master Summary form

SQUEEZE SPENDING PLAN (SSP) SUMMARY

Month/Yr. MASTER End Date 1/28/2011 Weeks 4

INCOME	PLAN	ACTUAL	DIFFERENCE
INCOME	3,000		
LAST MONTH - Positive Bottom Line			
TOTAL INCOME	3,000		
EXPENSES	**PLAN**	**ACTUAL**	**DIFFERENCE**
LAST MONTH - Negative Bottom Line			
(1) DEBITS / CHECKS			
(2) CASH ____ x ____ (# of weeks, dollars/wk)			
(3) CREDIT CARD PAYMENTS			
(4) FLEXIBLE SPENDING MONEY			
(5) SAVINGS / INVESTMENTS			
TOTAL EXPENSES			
BOTTOM LINE	**PLAN**	**ACTUAL**	**DIFFERENCE**
(Income minus Expenses)			

NOTE: Harvey has decided to start a *Squeeze* Spending Plan and he has agreed to let us follow his progress. He has also promised to keep an open mind. This icon will appear on each of his SSP's and worksheets. This is the first installment.

CHAPTER FOUR

SPYING ON YOUR SPENDING

"Money is always there, but the pockets change."
– Gertrude Stein

"So spy on yours to be sure it only leaves your pockets if you truly want it to."
– Patricia Stallworth

Squeeze Principle #3: Living within your means will keep you out of debt. Living beneath your means could make you rich!

If you've ever wondered where all of your money goes, there's an easy way to find out—spy on it! And it's not as difficult as you might think.

Taking Clues from *How* You Spend Your Money to Take Control and Simplify Your Finances

You generally make purchases in one of three ways: cash, debit cards (or checks), or credit cards (the Big 3). Each of these has a direct impact on your bottom line—debits and checks come directly out of your account immediately, cash comes out of your pockets, and credit card charges are eventually paid with money from your bank account. However, since there are only three major ways to spend your money, you can monitor your spending habits, and by just shifting the way you pay for purchases, you can control your money, and greatly simplify your finances. For example, studies show that people who use credit cards for purchases tend to spend more and purchase more items, so if you use credit cards only for emergencies, you have the opportunity to cut not only cut your expenses but to eliminate the need to spend extra money in the form of interest charges with just one tiny shift. And if you think the studies are wrong, watch your own behavior when you pay with cash versus using a card. See if you tend to pick up more items or not be as concerned with the price when you pay with a card as you are with cash.

On the other hand, using cash for more purchases allows you to cut down on the number of debits or checks you have to manage and that can simplify your finances. So learning how to manipulate the Big 3 can both save you money and simplify your life.

Because *how* you spend your money is so important to staying in control, it's the main focus of the *Squeeze* Spending Plan (SSP). While how much you pay for purchases is also important, the first line in controlling your spending is looking at how you spend your money. And being in control ultimately reduces your money stress. Once you get a clear picture of the *how*, you can then focus on being a savvy shopper, eliminating wasteful spending, and keeping your expenses in line with your income and goals.

TRACKING THE 'BIG 3'

How you spend your money provides the best clues to control it, and the *Squeeze* Spending Plan (SSP) looks at each of the 'Big 3' in detail—debits/checks, cash, and credit cards. Each of these spending methods plays a different role in customizing your Spending Plan, and as a result, they are listed separately. We will cover debits/ checks and cash in this chapter. Credit cards will be discussed in Chapters 5. The *Squeeze* Spending Plan uses these in the following ways:

- ***Debits/Checks***, including online banking and automatic bill payments, are used to pay bills, make credit card payments, add to savings, or pay for any remaining purchases.
- ***Cash*** is used for ordinary expenses like food, lunches, and other small miscellaneous purchases.
- ***Charges*** or credit cards are used for convenience and as a cash management tool to shift unexpected payments from one month to the next.

Recurring Debits and Checks: Tracking Your General Living Expenses

Your biggest expenses each month are most likely for core lifestyle expenses that don't vary much from month to month. These expenses are the easiest to predict because, in most cases, you receive a bill or an e-mail notification of the payment amount at about the same time each month, and you probably pay them with either with a debit card, a check, a bank authorization, or through online banking services. These generally include items like your rent or mortgage, utilities, auto payments, cable, etc. However, they may also include items that you don't receive a bill for, such as church offerings.

IDENTIFYING YOUR RECURRING PAYMENTS

Using the *Debits/Checks Worksheet* on the next page, check off the items you pay. The worksheet includes several different types of expenses, but if you don't see one you pay, add it to the list. Then enter the bill amount in the Monthly Plan column. For bills you pay less often than monthly, break them down into monthly payments. For example, if you make quarterly payments for health insurance or estimated tax payments, divide the quarterly payment by three to get to a monthly figure. Next, include how often you pay the bill (monthly, quarterly, annually, etc.) and the due date. Use your check register and statements to help you remember them all, especially bills that you pay less often than monthly. You can use an estimate for those bills that vary monthly like utilities, but ***do not*** list credit card payments *(we will cover those in Chapter 5).*

Also, include items you pay regularly but you do not receive a bill for such as church donations, music lessons, etc. The key is to list all payments that are constant and predictable so you cover the basics before you move on to other sections of the plan.

Squeeze: Debits/Checks Worksheet

Instructions: List all of the recurring bills you pay with debits, checks, online, or with authorized withdrawals. Do not include credit card payments. Use the categories or rename them to fit your needs.

NAME	MONTHLY PLAN	MONTHLY ACTUAL	DIFFERENCE	HOW OFTEN[1]	DUE DATE
☐ Rent/Mortgage					
☐ Car Payment					
☐ Home Phone					
☐ Cell Phone					
☐ Cable					
☐ Utilities					
☐ Gas					
☐ Electric					
☐ Water					
☐ Garbage					
☐ HOA					
☐ Church					
☐ Insurance					
☐ Life Insurance					
☐ Car Insurance					
☐ Health Insurance					
☐ Homeowners Insurance					
☐ Home Equity Loan					
☐ Student Loans					
☐ Prescriptions					
☐					
☐					
☐					
TOTAL					

[1] monthly, quarterly, annually, etc.

Hey, wait a minute. I pay my credit cards online every month. Why don't you want me to list them as a recurring bill?

Good question, Harvey. We are not including credit card payments here because we need to collect more information about them. We are devoting a whole chapter to them so I promise we will give you credit for your payments.

Managing Your Expenses as a Couple

If you haven't already done so, make a decision about how you want to manage your expenses as a couple. Will you put all of your money in one account? Or will you have a special account for household expenses that you both contribute to and keep everything else separate? One decision is not necessarily better than the other, but it will affect how you use the *Squeeze* Spending Plan. For example, if you are pooling all of your money in one account, you can follow the plan as is. However, if you will both contribute to a special household account decide the types of bills the account will cover and if you will split the bills 50/50 or if you will contribute proportionately based on your income.

Dividing Expenses Proportionally Based on Your Income

	You	Your Partner	Total
Monthly Income	\$3,000	\$2,000	\$5,000
Joint Household Bills %	3,000 ÷ 5,000 = 60%	2,000 ÷ 5,000 = 40%	100%

Ask for Account Alerts & Duplicate Checks: If you and your spouse use the same account, chances are not all ATM withdrawals get recorded, so ask for account alerts so you don't get caught off guard. Many banks offer these so that when your account drops below a certain balance, they will alert you so you can avoid overdraft fees. Also if you use checks, ask your bank for duplicate checks. Since most banks no longer return checks, duplicate checks allow you to make a carbon copy of every check you write. This way you will always have a receipt handy if you need it.

ADDING DEBITS/CHECKS TO YOUR MASTER SSP

Once you complete the *Debits/Checks Worksheet,* total the amounts listed in the Monthly Plan column and enter that total on your MASTER SSP Summary worksheet in the EXPENSE section in the PLAN column of (1) DEBITS/ CHECKS. *(See Harvey's worksheet below and Summary SSP on p. 64)*

Harvey's Debits/Checks Worksheet

Squeeze: Debits/Checks Worksheet 1/2011

NAME	MONTHLY PLAN	MONTHLY ACTUAL	DIFFERENCE	HOW OFTEN[1]	DUE DATE
Rent/Mortgage	750			monthly	1
Cell Phone	80			monthly	1
Utilities	60			monthly	1
Gas Credit Card	160			monthly	15
Church	100			monthly	
Car Insurance	75			monthly	1
Renters Insurance	8			annual $96	2/20
Health Insurance	219			monthly	1
Estimated Tax Payments	415			quarterly	3/6/9/12
TOTAL	1,867				

Note: Harvey is treating his gas credit card as a recurring expense because he pays it off each month.. Also, see Harvey's updated plan on p. 64.

Go Green: The Cash Factor

Studies show that people who use cash for purchases not only spend less than people who use credit cards or even debit cards, but they purchase fewer items. I believe this has something to do with the pain associated with handing over real dollars as opposed to just swiping a card. Yet fewer people are using cash today, and they are opting to use cards instead. Unfortunately, the switch to credit and debit cards, while convenient, is actually making the process of managing your money tougher because it creates a disconnect between you any your money, and makes it easier to spend more money than you may have actually planned, and in some cases than you actually have. On the other hand, using cash is the ultimate way to keep your spending on track because when it's gone, that's a signal to stop spending.

Ah, the Simplicity of Cash

Jennifer has set aside $30 for lunches in her spending plan. She decided on this amount so that she can save for a new car. But instead of using cash, she uses a credit card to pay for her lunches. Here is how her first week went: On Monday she spent $10 (she was okay until a dessert near the register caught her eye). On Tuesday she spent $8. On Wednesday and Thursday she spent $6, and she spent a whopping $15 on Friday because she were having a really bad day. Her total for the week—$45! If she continues this way she will end up spending $180 for the month versus the $120 she had originally planned to spend. And, her lunches could get even more expensive if she doesn't pay off her credit card bill and interest starts to add up.

Davis, on the other hand, also sets aside $30 to spend on lunches each week but he uses cash. He too has a goal to purchase a new car and he plans to make it happen so he vows that when his money is gone it's gone and he will have to make due until the next week. However, just in case of emergency, he has lots of peanut butter and jelly on hand.

Hey, wait a minute. I hear you, and I have been there, but I don't like the idea of carrying cash around. Are there any other ways that I can accomplish the same thing because I know I'm overspending?

Sure. One option is to set up a special debit card just for "cash." In other words, you transfer the amount you want to spend each month to that card. However, since you don't have the actual cash to stop you from spending more than you have available, you will need to track your spending each week to be sure you're staying on track. You can do this by using a debit card register, available at some banks and on the *Squeeze* website, or you can attach a sticky note to the front of your card so it is easy to record each purchase every time you use the card.

Creating a Cash Strategy for Everyday Expenses

Everyday expenses are expenses that occur every month. Like the bills in your debits/checks expense category, these expenses generally don't vary that much from month to month, so they are also predictable like your general living expenses. They include things like food, eating out, general entertainment, and drugstore items. To determine how much cash you will need for your everyday expenses during the month, start by estimating the amount you spend on items like those just mentioned in an average week. The goal is to have enough cash during the week to cover your everyday expenses so that you don't have to use one of the other two major forms of payment (debits/checks or credit cards) for purchases. The more often you use cash, the less time you will have to spend tracking and managing your accounts.

The *Cash Worksheet* on p. 58 includes some suggested categories to use in determining your cash expenses. However, space has been provided for you to add your own categories to the worksheet. Complete the worksheet by estimating your expenses in each category each week. Here are some additional details about each category:

- **Food** – if you split your eating between home and restaurants, your CASH can be used to cover all food. On the other hand, if you mostly eat at home, you may want to consider groceries an item to pay by debit card or check and include a monthly amount for it on your *Debits/Checks Worksheet.* Then you can reserve your weekly CASH to cover dinners out.
- **Gas** – Include the amount you need to fill your tank each week, unless you charge all of your gas. If you charge your gas, you can include the payment for your gas charges as a recurring payment on your *Debits/ Checks Worksheet. (See Harvey's worksheet p. 53)*
- **Fun/Entertainment** – What's fun and entertainment to you? This can be anything. Choose an amount you generally spend monthly.

- **Drugstore** – This is primarily for your current needs. However, if you want to stock up on occasion, it's okay to use more than one week's allotment, but be sure to write yourself a reminder so you don't overspend.
- **Lunches** – If you eat out for lunch, you probably already set aside a certain amount of cash for these purchases.
- **Small Miscellaneous** – This includes purchases of $50 or less, such as personal grooming, dry cleaning, car washes, etc.

In general, take a good look at your lifestyle, and design your use of cash around it. The goal is to build consistency in using the same amount each week or at least each month.

Once you have some estimates, complete the *Cash Worksheet* on the next page. Next, total the monthly amount and divide it by four to get an average weekly amount. Then pick a day of the week to *get paid*. This will be the day of the week that you collect your cash for the coming week. Pick a day that works well with your schedule. Friday is a traditional choice, but you can choose any day that works for you.

BOTTOM LINE ... HOW YOU SPEND YOUR CASH IS UP TO YOU. YOU CAN SPEND IT AS PLANNED OR ON SOMETHING TOTALLY DIFFERENT.

Lastly, test this amount over the next four weeks to be sure it's a reasonable amount for you. If you find yourself constantly dipping into the next week, track your expenses for two weeks by writing down everything that you spend your cash on. This should allow you to determine if you didn't allow enough or if you are overspending. Once you have the right weekly amount, think of it as a fixed expense, and keep it constant. Over time your spending patterns will adjust to the level you choose.

ADDING CASH TO YOUR MASTER SSP

Once you complete the *Cash Worksheet* and you have a weekly average amount you will need, you can add it to your Summary SSP. Using your Summary SSP, place the number of weeks in the month on the line next to (2) CASH and then place the weekly amount on the next line. Finally, multiply the two numbers together and place that number in the PLAN column. *(See Harvey's worksheet on SSP on p. 63-64)*

Squeeze: Cash Worksheet

Instructions: List all of your recurring weekly expenses by week. Total all of the weekly totals and divide by four to get a weekly average.

ITEM	Week #1	Week #2	Week #3	Week #4	MONTHLY PLAN	MONTHLY ACTUAL	DIFFERENCE
Food							
Groceries							
Dining Out							
Gas							
Fun/Entertainment							
Drug Store Items							
Lunches							
Small Miscellaneous							
MONTHLY TOTAL							
WEEKLY TOTAL *(monthly total ÷ by 4)*							

Hey, wait a minute. What if something comes up and I spend more money one week or I run out of money before the end of the month?

You're right. Life is not always easy to predict. But, remember, your cash is just for typical expenses that occur each month. If you overspend one week, deduct that amount from the next week. So if you have $100 to spend for the week and you spend $120, deduct $20 from the next week. This means you will only have $80 to spend the next week. If it is close to end of the month and you have no cash left, you can visit the ATM and get $20 to tide you over until you get paid. But keep in mind that that $20 will need to be deducted from your money next month. I know this may sound harsh, but you are selecting the amount of CASH you need, and the goal is to stay within your allocations. So overspending one week means that you have to under spend the next week to stay on track.

If you find that you are constantly overspending, it may mean that you have not allocated enough cash for your expenses or that your expenses are not in line with your income, and they need to be adjusted.

Simplify the Process Even More

Label four envelopes ***Week1, Week2, Week3, and Week4.*** Then get the total amount of cash you need for the month in one trip to the bank and place the appropriate amount in each envelope. This allows you to start each week with cash and to avoid the worry of trying to stay within the amount you selected.

A Tip about Tips:

If you earn tips on your job, instead of just letting them slip away, use them as a part of your weekly cash amount. If the amount you earn in tips is less than the amount you need weekly, add enough to bring it up to the level you need. On the other hand, if you earn more in tips than you need for the week, place the extra dollars in an envelope for the next week.

SQUEEZE POINTS:

- ***Squeeze Principle #3: Living within your means will keep you out of debt. Living beneath your means could make you rich!***
- You spend money in three basic ways: debits/checks, cash, and credit cards. Monitoring your spending in these three key areas allows you to understand your spending patterns and to make shifts to control and/or simplify your financial life.
- The *Squeeze* Spending Plan is based on *how* you spend your money. Then once you understand and take control of the *how*, you can focus on being a savvy shopper and on the *how much* part of the formula.
- Recurring debits/checks are generally used to support your lifestyle. They include payments for items like your rent/mortgage, utilities, auto loans, etc. They are the easiest to predict because you generally receive a bill or an e-mail notification when they are due. These payments represent the first type of expenses listed in

SQUEEZE POINTS *(continued):*

the *Squeeze* Spending Plan.

- It's a fact people who use cash spend less. And as an added benefit, using cash can greatly simplify your financial life because it eliminates the need to track and manage it. Finally, using cash for ordinary weekly expenses means that you can't overspend, and you always know how much money you have at all times. Some areas to use cash for purchases include food, fun or entertainment, lunches, drugstore items, and occasional items like personal grooming, dry cleaning, and car washes.

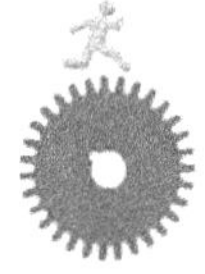

***SQUEEZE* ACTION ITEMS:**

1. Spy on your spending for the next two weeks. Write down everything you purchase in a journal, a check register, or notebook. List the date, item, the amount and whether you paid with cash, a check, a debit card, or a credit card. Then, at the end of two weeks, review your list. This information will not only come in handy as you create your spending plan, but it should also provide you with some added insights into your spending priorities and behaviors.

Continued on the next page

SQUEEZE ACTION ITEMS (continued)

2. Using the *Debits/Checks Worksheet,*[1] compile a list of all of the bills you either pay with a debit card, by check, online, or have automatic payments set up. Next, complete the Monthly Plan amount, how often you pay the bill, and the due date columns. **Do not include credit card payments**. Place a copy in your binder.
3. Using your MASTER SSP Summary form, locate (1) DEBITS/CHECKS in the EXPENSES section and transfer the total from your Debits/Checks Worksheet to the column titled PLAN.
4. Complete the *Cash Worksheet*[1] by compiling a list of your monthly cash expenses. Then divide your total for the month by four to get an average weekly amount. Place a copy in your binder.
5. Using your Master SSP copy, locate (2) CASH in the EXPENSES section, and transfer the number of weeks in the month (you can get this from your annual calendar that highlights your pay days) and the average weekly amount to the appropriate space. Then multiply the two numbers together to get the monthly amount and place the total in the column titled PLAN.
6. Pick a day of the week to get paid. This will be the day that you get your next stash of cash for the coming week.

**See Harvey's worksheets on p. 53 and 63, and his Master SSP on p 64.*

[1] Blank copies are available at www.squeezeyourmoney.com.

SQUEEZE STORY:

Stella and Cara

As a single mom, it hasn't always been easy for me, and I certainly don't want that for my daughter, Cara. She recently graduated from college—the first in our family to go to college, and I'm so proud of her. But I also worry because of all the money she borrowed to go to school she will end up like me—living paycheck to paycheck. She tells me not to worry. She says it will be okay, but how can I not worry. I know how tough it is to always be in debt and always having to play catch up.

Harvey's Cash Worksheet

Squeeze: Cash Worksheet 1/2011 

ITEM	Week #1	Week #2	Week #3	Week #4	MONTHLY PLAN	MONTHLY ACTUAL	DIFFERENCE
Food	50	50	50	50	200		
Groceries							
Dining Out							
Gas							
Fun/Entertainment	25	25	25	25	100		
Drug Store Items	55						
Lunches	25	35	40	25	125		
Small Miscellaneous				40	40		
MONTHLY TOTAL	155	110	115	140	465		
WEEKLY TOTAL *(monthly total ÷ by 4)*					116		

Harvey's updated SSP Summary

SQUEEZE SPENDING PLAN (SSP) SUMMARY

Month/Yr. MASTER   End Date 1/28/2011   Weeks 4

INCOME	PLAN	ACTUAL	DIFFERENCE
INCOME	3,000		
LAST MONTH - Positive Bottom Line			
TOTAL INCOME	3,000		
EXPENSES	**PLAN**	**ACTUAL**	**DIFFERENCE**
LAST MONTH - Negative Bottom Line			
(1) DEBITS / CHECKS	1,867		
(2) CASH 4 (# of weeks) x $116 (dollars/wk)	464		
(3) CREDIT CARD PAYMENTS			
(4) FLEXIBLE SPENDING MONEY			
(5) SAVINGS / INVESTMENTS			
TOTAL EXPENSES			
BOTTOM LINE	**PLAN**	**ACTUAL**	**DIFFERENCE**
(Income minus Expenses)			

CHAPTER FIVE

PUTTING CREDIT IN A SPECIAL PLACE

"Money talks – but credit has an echo."
– Bob Thaves

"Like the interest payments you make each month to rent credit!"
– Patricia Stallworth

Squeeze Principle #4: A credit limit does not represent money you have available, so resist the temptation to act like it does!

Using credit cards is the third big way your money leaves you. Credit cards make it easy and convenient to purchase items, and they make a great backup in case of an emergency. *That is,* when you control them. But when they control you, it's a whole different story. If you're like many people who depend on credit cards, one of the first things that comes to mind before using a credit card is whether or not you have enough room on your card and how a specific purchase will affect your monthly payment, but not the real cost.

The Real Cost of Credit

The real cost of using credit—a promise to repay a loan

plus interest with future dollars—is much bigger than the cost of the item plus interest. It's also the lost opportunity to invest that money and have it grow over time. To get an idea of your real cost of using credit cards, add up all of your credit card payments each month and imagine that instead of sending those dollars off to the credit card company that you're investing them. So if you have monthly credit card payments of $325, and you invest that amount and earn 8 percent, at the end of 40 years, you would have $1 million. That's your lost opportunity cost.

The goal of this chapter is to develop a picture of the role that credit cards play in your life. Once you see the whole picture, you can determine if you like what you see, or if you would like to take steps to lower your credit card debt. If so, you will have the majority of the information you need to develop a get-out-of-debt plan like the one outlined in Chapter 15.

How to Use Credit in a Healthy Spending Plan

Aside from the convenience that credit cards provide, they can also be an effective tool to use when debit cards, checks, or cash either aren't accepted or it's too risky to use them, such as with some online purchases or large purchases like airline tickets. And they can also be used to spread out the payments when you have an emergency and you don't have the dollars available to pay the bill when it arrives. So credit cards have a place in a healthy spending plan. The difference between having a credit card that *helps* you and one that *hurts* you is *how* you use it, so I'm a strong advocate of planning credit card purchases the same way you plan your cash and debit purchases. In other words, coordinate purchases with your income so that you have the funds available to pay the bill when it arrives. This is how some people are able to use credit cards to pay their regular bills and get the benefits of adding points to their programs without adding to their credit card balances. Credit cards deserve their own special place in your spending plan so that you will always know where you stand in this category. When you lump them in with your other expenses, this information is often lost, and along with it, the opportunity to manage or *squeeze* the most out of every dollar.

Creating Your Credit Card Profile

Using the *Credit Card Payments Worksheet* on the next page, list all of your open credit cards, charge cards, department store, and gas cards, including the company name, the outstanding balance, the current interest rate, the due date, and the minimum monthly payment. Next, place the minimum payment amount or the amount you plan to pay in the column titled Monthly Plan. If you're unsure about the amount you want to pay, put the minimum payment amount in the column and your *Squeeze* Spending Plan (SSP) will show you if there are extra dollars available to put toward paying down your balance. However, if you normally pay your credit cards off each month, put the entire balance in the Monthly Plan column.

Finally, total the Outstanding Balance column and the Monthly Plan columns. If you have never totaled your outstanding balances before, this number could be shocking, but it is a number you should always know.

Listing your credit cards separately has three major benefits: first, it allows you to see the total of how much money you owe; second, it allows you to see the percentage of your income that is being directed toward credit card payments as compared to your other expenses; and third, it provides you with the information, and in many cases, the motivation to make changes.

Squeeze: Credit Card Payments Worksheet

Instructions: List all of your open credit cards, charge cards, department store, and gas cards. Also, include the outstanding balance, interest rate, due date and minimum payment. Then list either the minimum payment or the amount you plan to pay in the Monthly Plan column.

Name	BALANCE	INTEREST RATE	DUE DATE	MINIMUM PAYMENT	MONTHLY PLAN	ACTUAL	DIFFERENCE
exp. VISA	*5,000*	*17.9*	*15*	*125*	*200*		
TOTAL							

ADDING CREDIT CARD PAYMENTS TO YOUR MASTER SSP SUMMARY

Once you complete the *Credit Card Payments Worksheet,* total the Monthly Plan column and transfer the total to your Master SSP EXPENSE category labeled (3) CREDIT CARD PAYMENTS. *(See Harvey's SSP on p. 70.)*

Squeeze Points:

- ***Squeeze Principle #4: A credit limit does not represent money you have available, so resist the temptation to act like it does!***
- The real cost of credit goes far beyond just repaying the amount you borrowed plus interest. It's really the opportunity lost by not having that money available to invest for your future. Imagine investing it instead of sending it off to credit card companies. Investing $200 or more each month can add up to a large sum of money in ten, twenty, or thirty years.
- There is a role for credit cards in a healthy spending plan. One is to serve as a cash management tool so you can extend the payments if you have an emergency and you don't have the funds available to cover it.

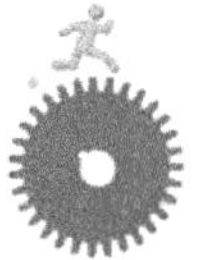

Squeeze Action Items:

1. Gather your latest credit card statements and complete the *Credit Card Payments Worksheet*. Place a copy in your binder.
2. Using your Master SSP form, locate (3) CREDIT CARD PAYMENTS in the EXPENSES section and transfer the total from your *Credit Card Payments Worksheet* to the PLAN column.

* Blank copies of worksheets are available at www.squeezeyourmoney.com.

Harvey's Credit Card Payments Worksheet and updated Master SSP

Squeeze: Credit Card Payments Worksheet

CARD NAME	BALANCE	INTEREST RATE	DUE DATE	MINIMUM PAYMENT	MONTHLY PLAN	MONTHLY ACTUAL	DIFFERENCE
VISA	1,500	19.9	1	60	60		
MasterCard	850	14.9	15	34	40		
TOTAL	2,350			94	100		

SQUEEZE SPENDING PLAN (SSP) SUMMARY

Month/Yr. MASTER End Date 1/28/2011 Weeks 4

INCOME	PLAN	ACTUAL	DIFFERENCE
INCOME	3,000		
LAST MONTH - Positive Bottom Line			
TOTAL INCOME	3,000		

EXPENSES	PLAN	ACTUAL	DIFFERENCE
LAST MONTH - Negative Bottom Line			
(1) DEBITS / CHECKS	1,867		
(2) CASH 4 (# of weeks) x $116 (dollars/wk)	464		
(3) CREDIT CARD PAYMENTS	100		
(4) FLEXIBLE SPENDING MONEY			
(5) SAVINGS / INVESTMENTS			
TOTAL EXPENSES			

BOTTOM LINE	PLAN	ACTUAL	DIFFERENCE
(Income minus Expenses)			

CHAPTER SIX

PLANNING FOR FLEXIBLE SPENDING

"Beware of little expenses: a small leak will sink a great ship."

– Benjamin Franklin

"And a plan that doesn't allow for everyday expenses will soon start leaking."

– Patricia Stallworth

Squeeze Principle #5: Stress your money, not yourself. Always keep a stash of cash on hand in case of an emergency!

What's flexible spending? Flexible spending basically means allowing money in your plan for the expenses that show up sooner or later in everyone's life but don't quite fit into general living or everyday expenses. These include things like clothing, medical and dental bills, birthday gifts, and car registration fees, just to mention a few, and if you don't allow for these, they could hinder your ability to control your spending and cause your plan to be off month after month. Since the priority and cost of these expenses varies from month to month, flexibility is essential.

Flexible Spending Money

Flexible Spending Money is generally used for occasional or out of the ordinary expenses and emergencies as well as for fun or spontaneous spending. Flexible Spending Money has three main components—expected expenses that you can plan for, like annual auto registrations; unexpected expenses that you can't plan for, like a trip to the emergency room for a minor injury; and money to enjoy, whether it's a planned outing or one that comes up at the last minute like an impromptu dinner with friends. When you know about a purchase in advance, you can either save for it over time or you can plan to make the purchase in a month with enough Flexible Spending Money available to cover it. And when an emergency arises (something you did not plan for and you do not have the money for), you can plan the payments to fit into future months' Flexible Spending Money by working out a payment plan or using a credit card.

> FLEXIBLE SPENDING MONEY IS TYPICALLY USED FOR KNOWN EXPENSES, EMERGENCIES, AND FUN & SPONTANEOUS SPENDING.

PLANNING FOR EXPECTED EXPENSES

Every year certain events occur that you can count on just like clockwork—you get your car serviced, you go to the doctor, and your favorite store has an annual sale. And even though you know they're coming, they can still catch you off guard or stress your wallet when they happen. So the best solution is to plan for these known events in advance, and one way to do that is to take an annual calendar and fill-in as many knowns as possible for each month. Begin by filling in birthdays, anniversaries, annual doctor/dentist visits, and anything else that generally comes up each year that you have to pay for. Also, include an estimate of the dollar amount. Then fill in new things that might be coming up such as a new furnace or appliance. *(See the example below.)*

List as many items as you can. Then use this information to help you decide how much Flexible Spending Money you will need each month for planned events. Advanced planning allows you to utilize all available resources. For example, planning your vacation in advance gives you the option to coordinate monies from your Savings, Flexible Spending Money, and Cash for the week to help spread the costs.

Use a calendar to plan for known expenses

January 2011

Sun	Mon	Tue	Wed	Thu	Fri	Sat
						1
2	3	4	5	6	7	8
9	10	11 Mom's Birthday $50	12	13	14	15
16	17	18	19	20	21 Car Service $195	22
23	24 Carl's Birthday $50	25	26	27	28	29
30	31					

PLANNING UNEXPECTED EXPENSES

Sometimes stuff just happens, stuff that you couldn't have predicted—you get sick and have to go to the emergency room, or some other type of emergency occurs without warning. And when emergencies occur, you may or may not have the funds available to cover them. If you have the extra funds, great! But if you don't, you may have to make other arrangements to pay for it, such as working out a payment plan with the hospital or using a credit card if you need to pay the bill in full immediately. In either case this is a bill that will need to be paid, and you can use your monthly Flexible Spending Money to make the payments until the balance is zero.

PLANNING FOR FUN AND SPONTANEOUS SPENDING

No matter how hard you try it's just not possible to stick with a spending plan that doesn't allow for fun or spontaneous spending. *Wants* seem to have a way of creeping up all the time. While they aren't necessities, our mind can sometimes trick us into thinking they are—things like concert tickets, a day of pampering at the spa, power tools, etc. It's important to provide Flexible Spending Money for some of these, or you can start to feel deprived, and when that happens, you could put your whole plan at risk by going on buying binges, or you could abandon it altogether. If you have enough money to cover all your wants, that's great, but if they exceed the amount you have available, start a Wish List. Every time you find yourself thinking, "I wish I had _______," write it down along with a realistic cost estimate. (See the *Wish List*

Worksheet on p. 76 for an example.) The more you write down, the better. Then as you are working on your SSP for the coming month, review your Wish List and decide which item or items from your list you want to buy.

CREATING A WISH LIST ALLOWS YOU TO STOP IMPULSE BUYING AND GET THE THINGS YOU REALLY WANT.

As an added bonus, creating a Wish List allows you to focus your spending on the items you still want after the initial urge has passed. Then as money becomes available, you can spend it on things you really want instead of watching it quickly disappear on impulse buys. After using your Wish List for a while, you may be surprised to see how many items you've purchased and how many you've crossed off because you no longer wanted them.

However, remember, not every *want* can be planned or anticipated so it's a good idea to always have a little cash cushion in your Flexible Spending Money bucket to accommodate unexpected good things. Things like dinner with friends, a special sale at your favorite store, or a weekend getaway so you don't have to miss out on these occasions or worse yet resort to charging your purchases without having the funds available to pay for them when the bill arrives. In other words, stay flexible, and remember that just because you have flexible money available, it doesn't mean you have to spend it all every month. In fact, you can accumulate your Flexible Spending Money for two or more months so that you can make a large future purchase with cash.

Squeeze: Wish List Worksheet

Instructions: Every time you find yourself thinking, "I wish I had __________," write it down along with a realistic cost estimate, the date and any notes regarding specifics or the location.

Item	Cost Estimate	Date	Notes/Location, etc.

How Much Is Enough?

How much money you include in your Flexible Spending Money category is most likely a moving target, changing from month to month as your needs change, so it's difficult to set an exact amount. However, ten percent of your take-home pay is a good place to start, and then you can adjust it up or down based on your specific situation. The more activities, possessions, and people in your life, the more Flexible Spending Money you are likely to need. For example, if you have two cars needing work, you will have twice the maintenance bills of someone with only one car. And likewise, a family of six has more flexible spending requirements than a family of two. So keep all of these factors in mind and make adjustments as needed. Start with your calendar of known expenses then add in additional money for emergencies and fun and spontaneous spending. Remember, you can always carry any leftover money over to the next month, add it to your Savings, or use it to decrease your credit card balances.

Using the *Flexible Spending Money Worksheet* on the next page, list any known expenses and the estimated amount you will need. Because Flexible Spending Money includes both planned and unplanned expenses, tracking your spending in this category can be helpful for future planning. An easy way to do this is to add the purchases and amounts you spend to a sticky note in your check register or by keeping your receipts and totaling them each week. If you have dollars left over at the end of the month or if you spend more than you allowed, these will be reflected in your SSP for the next month. (**Note:** We'll discuss more about how to do this in Chapter 9 when we discuss *Squeeze Your Money* monthly maintenance.)

Finally, remember that like *Cash*, how you spend your Flexible Spending Money is up to you. But there may be consequences down the road if you don't allocate funds for those expenses that will show up sooner or later, like your annual check up or a birthday gift for your mom.

ADDING FLEXIBLE SPENDING MONEY TO YOUR MASTER SSP

Once you complete the *Flexible Spending Money Worksheet*, total your known items for the month. Then add a cushion for emergencies and fun and spontaneous spending. Next locate (4) FLEXIBLE SPENDING MONEY on your Master SSP in the EXPENSES section and either enter the total amount from your *Flexible Spending Money Worksheet,* or if you prefer, start with ten percent of your take-home pay and place that amount in the PLAN column.

Squeeze: Flexible Spending Money Worksheet

Instructions: List all of your known expenses for the month. Also, review your wish list and add any additional purchases. Be sure to include a cushion for emergencies and spontaneous spending.

ITEM	Week #1	Week #2	Week #3	Week #4	MONTHLY PLAN	MONTHLY ACTUAL	DIFFERENCE
Example:. Birthday Gifts		*50*		*50*	*100*		
TOTAL							

SQUEEZE POINTS:

- ***Squeeze Principle #5: Stress your money, not yourself. Always keep a stash of cash on hand in case of an emergency!***
- Flexible Spending Money is money you allocate to cover known expenses that don't fit into any of the other expense categories, emergencies, and fun and spontaneous spending. The amount you allocate is based on a number of factors, including the number of possessions you have that might need repair or replacing, and the size of your family. For example,

Continued on the next page

SQUEEZE POINTS *(continued):*

families of five will most likely need more Flexible Spending Money than a couple.

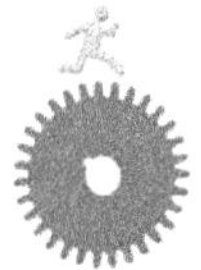

***SQUEEZE* ACTION LIST:**

1. Using an annual calendar, mark all of the typical expenses that occur during each month. Include things like car maintenance, doctor visits, birthdays, property taxes, etc. Then put a copy in your binder to serve as a reminder so you can plan for them. (**Note:** Purchase a small calendar or download a template from a site like www.microsoft.com.)
2. Enter known expenses for the coming month on the *Flexible Spending Money Worksheet*[1] along with a "fun money" amount or something from your Wish List as well as a cushion for emergencies. OR if you aren't sure how much to allocate to Flexible Spending Money, start with 10 percent of your take-home pay. Then using your Master SSP form, locate (4) FLEXIBLE SPENDING MONEY in the EXPENSES section and enter either the total from your *Flexible Spending Money Worksheet* or 10 percent of your monthly income in the PLAN column.
3. Start a Wish List[1] and keep it in your binder. Write down everything you want to buy as money becomes available and include a realistic cost estimate.

**See Harvey's worksheet and Master SSP on the next page.*

[1] Blank copies are available at www.squeezeyourmoney.com.

Harvey's Flexible Spending Worksheet and updated Master SSP

Squeeze: Flexible Spending Money Worksheet 

ITEM	Week #1	Week #2	Week #3	Week #4	MONTHLY PLAN	MONTHLY ACTUAL	DIFFERENCE
Birthday Gifts		50		50	100		
Car Service			195		195		
TOTAL					295		

SQUEEZE SPENDING PLAN (SSP) SUMMARY

Month/Yr. MASTER End Date 1/28/2011 Weeks 4

INCOME	PLAN	ACTUAL	DIFFERENCE
INCOME	3,000		
LAST MONTH - Positive Bottom Line			
TOTAL INCOME	3,000		

EXPENSES	PLAN	ACTUAL	DIFFERENCE
LAST MONTH - Negative Bottom Line			
(1) DEBITS / CHECKS	1,867		
(2) CASH 4 (# of weeks) x $116 (dollars/wk)	464		
(3) CREDIT CARD PAYMENTS	100		
(4) FLEXIBLE SPENDING MONEY	300		
(5) SAVINGS / INVESTMENTS			
TOTAL EXPENSES			

BOTTOM LINE	PLAN	ACTUAL	DIFFERENCE
(Income minus Expenses)			

CHAPTER SEVEN

SAVING FOR THE GOOD, THE BAD, AND THE UNEXPECTED

"It's not what you make, it's what you keep!"
— Unknown

"And the more you keep, the more choices you have!"
— Patricia Stallworth

Squeeze Principle #6: Savings are an essential part of every plan. Without savings you're doomed to live in an endless loop of ESS (earning, spending, and stressing) with no end in sight!

The ability to save at least a portion of the money you earn is extremely important if financial independence is one of your goals. Yet the average savings rate in the U.S. is less than 1 percent. The real key to growing your savings is to make it a priority and to save for a purpose. Saving for things you want, whether its retirement, a house, or a new outfit, will not only make saving easier, but it will keep you motivated when you're faced with temptations to spend your money on other things.

The Real Reason to Save

There are a ton of reasons why you should be a saver, but the biggest one of all is that having savings gives you choices—choices to build a secure future, to get the things you want, to take advantage of opportunities that come your way, or to cushion the blow if disaster hits. So if you haven't already started a savings plan, there is no time like the present, and there are two basic areas to start with—saving for the unexpected and saving for the good things in life.

Saving for the Unexpected

I'm starting with saving for the unexpected first because having an emergency fund is one of those essential elements that everyone needs but not many people think about until you it's too late. Emergency funds are monies you have available to help you get back on your feet faster if something bad happens. And in many cases, they can help you stay on track by not jeopardizing your long-term investments or other goals.

Some things I consider major disasters include big auto repairs like a new engine, becoming ill for an extended period of time, or losing your job, and you can probably come up with your own list. The point is that without funds to bail yourself out, you could be in big trouble.

HOW MUCH MONEY SHOULD YOU KEEP IN YOUR EMERGENCY FUND?

While many people prefer to have a set amount available like $5,000 or $10,000, others prefer to aim for an amount based on the expenses they would like to cover. The level you choose to keep will depend on a number of factors, including how secure you are in your job as well as the types of insurance you have to supplement your income should you become ill, for example. A general rule of thumb is to accumulate enough money to cover three to six months of expenses. However, you should consider your situation in choosing an amount. If there is a possibility that you could lose your job, you will want to accumulate enough to last until you can most likely find another one. Or if your income is seasonal or has wild fluctuations, you might want to have more months of savings available to cover your expenses. To calculate an amount based on your actual expenses, use the *Emergency Fund Goal Worksheet* below.

Squeeze: Emergency Fund Goal Worksheet

Instructions: Using the information from your spending plan, calculate the amount of money you will need to save to cover your expenses for a set number of months. A general rule of thumb is three to six months of expenses, however, you can choose any number you feel comfortable with based on your situation.

	amount/mo		# of months	
(1) DEBITS/CHECKS	________	×	________	________
(2) CASH	________	×	________	________
(3) CREDIT CARDS	________	×	________	________
(4) OTHER	________	×	________	________
TOTAL				

In addition to building an emergency fund from scratch, you can also use other resources you have to supplement your fund in case of a real emergency. Use the *Emergency Fund Resources* worksheet on the next page to calculate the amount you would have available. While using investments slated for other goals should not be your first line of

Squeeze: Emergency Fund Resources

Instructions: Calculate the amount of money you would have available in case of an emergency.

Resource	Amount Available	When Available
❑ Cash on hand	$	Immediate
❑ Checking account	$	Immediate
❑ Savings account	$	Immediate
❑ Money market account	$	Immediate
❑ Current lines of credit	$	Immediate
❑ Credit card cash advance	$	Immediate
❑ CDs	$	1 business day
❑ Mutual funds	$	3 to 5 business days
❑ Checking account	$	Immediate
❑ Brokerage account	$	3 to 5 business days
❑ Liquidating other investments	$	
❑ Getting a bank loan	$	
❑ Borrowing from family/friends	$	
❑ Borrowing from your 401(k)	$	5 to 10 business days
Total from all reliable resources	$	

defense, it's good to know all of the resources you have available and how long it would take to make them available if a real emergency occurred.

Finally, avoid dipping into it your emergency fund for non-emergency items, and if you do need to take money out, consider it a loan and replace it as soon as possible.

WHERE SHOULD YOU KEEP YOUR EFUND?

It's important to have your emergency fund in investments that you can dip into at any time with little or no loss of principal. In other words, "*safe*" investments like savings accounts, CDs, and money market accounts and funds (the type you get from a mutual fund company or a brokerage firm). If you opt for a savings or money market account at your credit union or bank, you may want to also consider money market funds or other types of safe mutual funds as your cash grows for at least a portion of your money so that you can earn more interest. *(Note: For more ideas on places to grow and keep your emergency fund, see Chapter 13).*

THE REALLY GOOD THING ABOUT AN EFUND

Generally when you think of an emergency fund, you think of having something to help you bounce back when disaster hits, but emergency funds can also be used for unexpected good things that happen to you as well. It can be used for things like business opportunities that come from out of the blue, and you can use them to so good things for yourself and your family, however you define that. In either case, remember, the main function is to serve as a cushion so if you take money out, put it back as quickly as possible.

RESOURCES & TERMS

Terms

money market accounts: Accounts you set up at a bank or a credit union and they are FDIC insured.

Continued on the next page

RESOURCES & TERMS (continued)

money market funds: Accounts you set up at a mutual fund company or brokerage firm and they are not guaranteed.

safe investments a.k.a. capital preservation investments: Accounts that focus on preserving the amount of your investment or principal. Examples include savings accounts and money market accounts.

Saving for the Good Stuff

The good stuff is anything that's important to you. And it's hard to talk about saving for the good without talking about goals. Setting goals helps you get really specific about what it is you want, when you want it, and why you want it. And when you combine your goals with a plan to achieve them, you can become an unstoppable force like the *Doubling Pennies Game* on the next page.

If you already have a set of goals you're working on, you can continue to save for them in the *Squeeze* program. Use the *Savings/Investment Worksheet* on the next page. List your goals, the total amount you need, the current balance, the date you would like to have the funds, and the amount you want to save for the coming month. However, if you haven't started a savings program, get started by saving a portion of your income each month. Then as you set specific goals, you can shift your savings to them. If you don't have a specific amount in mind, ten percent of your income is a good place to start. Then you can adjust that amount up or down based on your needs and the amount of money you have available. Don't forget to consider any savings that are deducted from your paycheck.

For example, if you want to save 10 percent for retirement and 6 percent is deducted from your paycheck, you only need to save an additional 4 percent to reach your goal. *(Note: See Chapter 12 for more information on developing goals and a financial plan.)*

Squeeze: Savings/Investments Worksheet

Instructions: List your goals, including the total amount you need, the current balance, and the date you would like to have the money. Then put the current amount you want to invest in the Monthly Plan column.

GOAL	TOTAL AMOUNT NEEDED	CURRENT BALANCE	DATE NEEDED	MONTHLY PLAN	ACTUAL	DIFFERENCE
TOTAL						

Saving Really Works!

Q: How many days will it take to become a millionaire if a penny value doubles each day? The answer: 28 days! *(See the chart below.)*

1) .01	2) .02	3) .04	4) .08	5) .16	6) .32	7) .64
8) 1.28	9) 2.56	10) 5.12	11) 10.24	12) 20.28	13) 40.96	14) 81.92
15) 163.84	16) 327.68	17) 655.36	18) 1,310.72	19) 2,621.44	20) 5,242.88	21) 10,485.76
22) 20,971.52	23) 41,943.04	24) 83,886.08	25) 167,772.16	26) 335,544.32	27) 671,088.64	28) 1,342,177.28

While it might take you longer to achieve a goal like this, the principle is the same. Just get started and the more you add to your savings, the faster they will grow.

Start the Saving Habit Now!

Don't put it off another minute. Use the change in your pockets to get started and make a plan to add to it every day. Follow these three easy steps to get started:

1. Decide on one or more goals you want to accomplish and get a shoebox for each one.
2. Label the shoebox with the name of the goal. It could be something as simple as a new pair of shoes or as exotic as a Caribbean vacation.
3. Every night before you go to bed put something in each box, no matter how small. This will do two things. First, you will be saving for something you want and second, you will start to form a savings habit. And you know how hard it is to break habits. **Note:** This is also a great way to get your kids into the saving habit.

ADDING SAVINGS/INVESTMENTS TO YOUR MASTER SSP

Since your savings can be used for so many different purposes, it's more effective to have different buckets or accounts to fund your goals and emergencies. Start by completing the *Savings/Investments Worksheet,* or if you don't have any specific goals, start with a portion of your income, such as 10 percent. Once you have an amount for your monthly Savings/Investments category, locate (5) SAVINGS/INVESTMENTS in the EXPENSES section of your Master SSP and enter the amount from your worksheet or a percentage of your income.

SQUEEZE POINTS:

- ***Squeeze Principle #6: Savings are an essential part of every plan. Without savings you're doomed to live in an endless loop of ESS (earning, spending, and stressing) with no end in sight!***
- The first step in achieving financial independence is savings and it should always be a part of your spending plan. You don't need a ton of money to get started with a savings plan. Many mutual funds will let you get started with a small minimum investment, and Harriet's tip on p. 88 shows you how to get started with just the leftover change in your pockets.
- The real key to saving is to save for a purpose, whether it's an emergency fund to help you bounce back from unexpected things faster or savings to fund your goals.

SQUEEZE STORY:

Jackie and John

John handles all of the finances but I really think I should know more. My friend Theresa just lost her husband in an accident and she is lost because he handled everything. She doesn't even know what bills they owe and if the bills she's receiving are correct or if some are missing. I feel so bad for her.

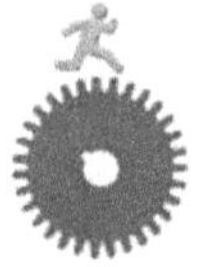

SQUEEZE ACTION ITEMS:

1. Complete the *Emergency Fund Goal Worksheet* (p. 83) and the *Emergency Fund Resources Worksheet* on (p. 84) and place a copy in your binder.
2. Complete the *SSP Savings/Investments Worksheet*[1] (p. 87) and place a copy in your binder. Include the goal, the amount needed, the current balance, and the date needed. If you don't already have one, don't forget to list an emergency fund as one of your goals.
2. Using your Master SSP copy, locate SAVINGS in the EXPENSES section and enter either the total from your Savings/Investments Worksheet or a percentage of your monthly income (such as 10 percent) in the PLAN column.
3. If you haven't already done so, open a separate savings account(s). Your savings should never be a part of your checking account or the account you use to pay bills.
4. If one of your goals is to save for retirement, read about the benefits of contributing to plans at work and IRAs on pp. 208-210 and 212. Your money will grow faster in these accounts because it grows tax-deferred, so it's worth looking into.

[1]Blank copies are available www.squeezeyourmoney.com

Harvey's Savings/Investments Worksheet and updated Master SSP

Squeeze: Savings/Investments Worksheet

GOAL	TOTAL AMOUNT NEEDED	CURRENT BALANCE	DATE NEEDED	MONTHLY PLAN	ACTUAL	DIFFERENCE
RE down payment	20,000	10,000	2/13	400		
Emergency fund	5,000	2,000				
TOTAL				400		

SQUEEZE SPENDING PLAN (SSP) SUMMARY

Month/Yr. MASTER   End Date 1/28/2011   Weeks 4

INCOME	PLAN	ACTUAL	DIFFERENCE
INCOME	3,000		
LAST MONTH - Positive Bottom Line			
TOTAL INCOME	3,000		
EXPENSES	**PLAN**	**ACTUAL**	**DIFFERENCE**
LAST MONTH - Negative Bottom Line			
(1) DEBITS / CHECKS	1,867		
(2) CASH 4 (# of weeks) x $116 (dollars/wk)	464		
(3) CREDIT CARD PAYMENTS	100		
(4) FLEXIBLE SPENDING MONEY	300		
(5) SAVINGS / INVESTMENTS	400		
TOTAL EXPENSES			
BOTTOM LINE	**PLAN**	**ACTUAL**	**DIFFERENCE**
(Income minus Expenses)			

Squeeze Story:

Sidney

I feel like I haven't stopped running since I graduated four years ago. I got a dream job at a major firm earning more money than I could imagine, and I'm hanging out with the "beautiful people." Not bad for a poor kid from the block. Unfortunately, that doesn't leave much time for anything else.

The other day I got a call from a bill collector, and I went into shock. I try to pay my bills on time, but I'm really short on time, and sometimes things do get lost. But I make so much money, how could this happen? I don't understand. I was upset, ashamed, and embarrassed at the same time. I'm really smart, and I should know what to do to get out of this mess, but I don't. A good friend who earns a lot less than I do and has no debt suggested that I add up all of my debts to get a look at how bad the problem was. I followed her suggestion, and I was really in shock after that. I can't believe I have been so foolish with my money. But that stops today. I never want to get another call from a bill collector. I'm going to stop ignoring my money. I'm going to find out how to get out of this mess and make my money to work for me because this just doesn't make any sense.

CHAPTER EIGHT

POLISHING YOUR PLAN

"Don't tell me where your priorities are. Show me where you spend your money and I'll tell you what they are."

— James Frick

"Like it or not, it's just that easy."

—Patricia Stallworth

All the numbers are in and it's time to finish your Master *Squeeze* Spending Plan (SSP).

Getting to the Bottom Line of Your Spending Plan

The last step in completing your Squeeze Spending Plan is calculating your Bottom Line. Start the process by totaling all of the expense categories (CHECKS, CASH, CREDIT CARD PAYMENTS, etc.) together and then enter the total at the bottom of the SSP next to TOTAL EXPENSES. Next, subtract your TOTAL EXPENSES from your TOTAL INCOME and enter this number in the BOTTOM LINE box. Be sure to recheck all of your numbers to make sure they are correct. How did you do? Is your Bottom Line positive, negative, or close to zero?

WORKING WITH A POSITIVE BOTTOM LINE

If you have a positive BOTTOM LINE or it is close to zero, you are basically finished. However you may want to review your SSP once again to be sure it reflects the way you want to spend your money. If it doesn't and you aren't able to make changes now, make notes for future changes such as increasing your savings level. On the other hand, if you have extra money, decide where it should go. You could use it to put more toward your Credit Card Payments, add to your Savings or your Flexible Spending Money. Likewise, if you are a few dollars short, choose the place(s) where you would like to cut back to avoid overspending.

WORKING WITH A NEGATIVE BOTTOM LINE

If you have a negative BOTTOM LINE—stop. Put brackets < > or parentheses ( ) around the amount so you don't confuse it for a positive number. Then keep working on your plan until your Bottom Line is zero or positive. However, instead of just making arbitrary cuts, go through each expense category and explore your options. Then make conscious cuts—cuts that make sense to you and cuts that you can live with. Start from the top of your of expenses and look for places to make cuts all the way down the list.

Making Spending Cuts

While you may not feel that there is any place that you can make cuts in your major expenses, don't cross the possibility off your list until you review each one. As you scan your expenses, look for ones where you might have some flexibility. There's probably not much you can do about your rent or mortgage payment short of moving, but you may be able to effectively cut that payment by getting a roommate. And conducting some simple research might reveal some flexibility in other areas and some pleasant surprises. For example, if it's been awhile since you got an auto or homeowner's insurance quote, now is a good time to look into those options. Go down the list and review every expense. Getting new quotes from your current company or competitors is one of the most painless ways to cut your spending. Next, determine if you are paying for subscriptions or cable services that you really don't use. If so, cancel them or get a package that is more inline with what you actually use. You can always go back if you decide to use them again in the future. Finally, look at minor expenses to see if there are places you can cut or scale back. If you have a family, be sure to get them involved in the process as well.

GETTING NEW QUOTES FROM YOUR CURRENT COMPANY OR COMPETITORS IS ONE OF THE MOST PAINLESS WAYS TO CUT YOUR SPENDING.

In either case, avoid making across-the-board cuts in areas like Savings and Flexible Spending Money. Savings are essential to achieve your goals and Flexible Spending Money is not just fun money. It also provides funding for those forgotten expenses that eventually show up like auto registrations and birthday gifts. These always seem to come at the worst possible time and they can put a real dent in your spending plan if you're not prepared for them. We started the Master Spending Plan with 10 percent in each of these categories and that might be too much for your situation at this time, so cut them if you need to, but don't cut them out altogether.

Also, be careful about skimping on your Cash. Most of the items in your Cash expenses are basic—food, gas, drugstore items, and some fun money. If you do decide to lower it, try to keep your weekly amount constant. Consistency is important to the plan so you get used to a certain amount of cash that you can depend on each week. As long as it's a reasonable amount for the level of expenses you have, your spending will eventually adjust to the new level and it will seem as though it was always that way.

Once you make changes, keep a close eye on them for three months to see if the cuts are working. If not, you may need to do some additional tweaking or if further cuts are not possible, you may need to look for ways to increase your income.

When the Numbers Say One Thing But Your Gut Says Another, Listen to Your Gut

Regardless of your BOTTOM LINE, if in your gut it just doesn't seem right, listen to your gut. An accurate Bottom Line is important because it will be used to make all sorts of money decisions and if it's wrong, it could lead you to make the wrong decisions.

Go back and review each item to make sure you have accounted for everything correctly. Here is a quick checklist you can follow:

Continued on the next page

When the Numbers Say One Thing... *(continued)*

INCOME

- ❑ **Did you record your gross income instead of your net?** Your gross income is the total amount you make before deductions. Your net is the actual amount you have available to spend. Always use your net income.
- ❑ **Verify your monthly income figures.** As a quick check, if you're paid weekly, multiply the amounts (gross and net) by 52, and then divide by 12. If you're paid bi-weekly, then multiply the gross and net amounts by 26, and then divide by 12.
- ❑ **Check to be sure you have included all of your income.** For example, do you receive child support or money from investments or a second job?
- ❑ **Did you record your payroll deductions accurately?** Are they all accounted for and are the amounts accurate?

EXPENSES

- ❑ **Did you include all of your debts?** Verify this again. Sometimes a spouse or partner has a debt that you may have forgotten about. Review all of your credit card statements and your check/debit register.
- ❑ **Have you accounted for all of your living expenses?** Don't forget about things like gifts to charity, cell phones, personal grooming, pet care, etc.
- ❑ **Did you include all of your automated payments?** Re-check insurance and other authorized withdrawals.
- ❑ **Have you included all of your occasional expenses?** Be sure you included expenses like property taxes, estimated taxes, and any other payments you may only have to pay occasionally.
- ❑ **Are you overstating any expenses?** For example, if you are behind in payments or you typically pay more than the minimum payment on your credit cards, use the minimum payment amount when creating your plan, so that you know the amount you will ordinarily owe. Then you can change the actual amount you pay on a monthly basis.

GENERAL EXPENSE GUIDELINES

If you are unsure about your expenses compare them to general recommended guidelines. Here are some guidelines to keep in mind as you review your expenses. Remember that everyone's situation is different, so don't worry if these don't fit you exactly, but aim to be somewhere in the ballpark:

- Housing expenses, including phone and utilities should be around one-third of your take-home pay.
- Food and transportation should be in the 15-percent range each.
- Clothing should be about 5 percent.

In other words, 60 to 70 percent of your take-home pay should cover your expenses. This leaves 30 to 40 percent to split between savings and investments, charity, entertainment and fun. While a minimum of 10 percent is recommended for savings and investments, you can divide the leftover amount any way you like.

General Expense Guidelines Chart

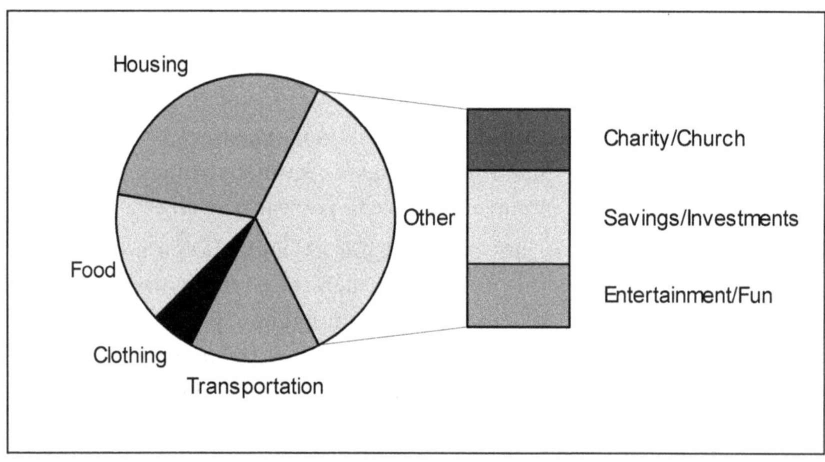

Why You Need a Cash Cushion

A cash cushion is a stash of cash you keep in your checking or savings account. You draw from it as needed throughout the month and it gets replenished as new income comes in. It serves two basic purposes:

1. To replace any shortfalls that may occur during the month. This will help prevent bounced checks and overdrafts, etc. While shortfalls can occur regardless of your situation, a cash cushion is essential if you have a fluctuating or unpredictable income. *(See p. 40 for more information on using a cash cushion with an unpredictable income.)*
2. To allow you to pay your bills when it is convenient for you, regardless of when you receive your income. This is especially helpful if you get paid more than once a month, because if you have enough of a cushion to cover your bills, you can pay them all at once instead of waiting until you get paid.

Hey, wait a minute. What's the difference between a Cash Cushion, a Cash Reserve, and an Emergency Fund, and do I need all of these?

Good question, Harvey. A *cash cushion* is money that you keep in your checking or savings. It's usually one month's expenses or less and the main purpose for having one is to cover any shortfalls you may have during the month in paying ordinary or predictable expenses.

On the other hand, an *emergency fund,* also known as a *cash reserve,* is mainly for unexpected emergencies that come up—emergencies like car repairs or hospital bills.

SQUEEZE POINTS:

- The last step in creating your Master *Squeeze* Spending Plan is to calculate your Bottom Line. This will result in one of three possibilities: it will be positive; it will be negative; or it will be zero. If it is positive or close to zero, you are basically finished. All you need to do is review your plan and decide where any remaining dollars should go. On the other hand, if it is negative, you will need to make cuts until it is zero or positive.
- If you need to make cuts in your expenses, avoid making across-the-board cuts in areas like Savings and Flexible Spending Money. Those are two important areas, so review every area and try to make cuts that you can live with for the long term.

SQUEEZE ACTION ITEMS:

1. Put the finishing touches on your plan. Add all up all of your expenses and subtract them from your income to determine your BOTTOM LINE. If it's positive, decide where you want to spend the extra money, and if it's negative keep working on it until you have a zero balance.
2. Review your expenses and spot check to see if you can cover all of your necessary expenses with 60 to 70 percent of your take-home pay. If not, compare the percentages you spend on each area with the

Continued on the next page

SQUEEZE ACTION ITEMS *(continued):*

guidelines on p. 98. Locate the areas where you are way off and look for ways to decrease your expenses so you can get closer to this overall percent.

(See Harvey's results below.)

So How Did Harvey Do?

Well, much to his surprise, Harvey ended up with a negative Bottom Line, and that was only making the minimum payments on his credit cards. *(See Harvey's before and after SSP's on pages 103 – 104.)* But it wasn't all bad. He was glad that he had done his initial spending on paper instead of watching his checks bounce. He quickly reworked some of his goals and spending, and then his plan was okay. Here is a summary of the changes Harvey decided to make:

1. He is concerned about his credit card debt and would like to pay it off as soon as possible. He has vowed not to charge anything else and always wants to pay more than the minimum when possible. His minimum payments are less than $100, and he has increased his payments to $200.

2. He wants to buy an income property, and he wants to save as much as possible for a down payment. His goal is to accumulate $10,000 in addition to the $10,000 he already has over the next two years for a total of $20,000. He set a savings goal of $400 per month but now realizes that he will have to increase his sales dramatically or look for a part-time job to reach that goal.

3. After some thought, he decided to cut his Flexible Spending Money to $200. He's single and feels that that is more than enough. And if he runs into a problem, he has his savings to fall back on.
4. Harvey increased his weekly Cash amount from $116 to $120. Easier access he said (ATM's dispense cash in multiples of $20) and he plans to put any remaining Cash or Flexible Money into Savings at the end of the month.

(See Harvey's before and after polishing SSP's on the next two pages.)

SQUEEZE STORY:

Joann and Michael

We're bracing for some major events. Our daughters, Sarah and Emily, will be going off to college in three years, and we're not sure what to do. Michael and I have made several attempts at saving for college, but there never seems to be anything left after we pay our bills, and what little we do manage to save always ends up being used for other things. Now we're in a panic because three years is not really that far away. We don't really want the girls to end up with huge student loans that will take forever to payoff, and we don't want to jeopardize our retirement, but the only real savings we have is in our 401(k). Friends tell us not to take money out of our 401(k), but I don't know what other choice we have.

Harvey's SSP *Before* Polishing:

SQUEEZE SPENDING PLAN (SSP) SUMMARY

Month/Yr. Master | End Date 1/28/2011 | Weeks 4

INCOME	PLAN	ACTUAL	DIFFERENCE
Income *(Take-home pay)*	3,000		
Income *(Take-home pay)*			
Other Income			
LAST MONTH - Positive Bottom Line			
TOTAL INCOME	3,000		

EXPENSES	PLAN	ACTUAL	DIFFERENCE
LAST MONTH - Negative Bottom Line			
(1) DEBITS / CHECKS	1,867		
(2) CASH 4 (# of weeks) x $116 (dollars/wk)	464		
(3) CREDIT CARD PAYMENTS	200		
(4) FLEXIBLE SPENDING MONEY	300		
(5) SAVINGS / INVESTMENTS	400		
TOTAL EXPENSES	3,131		

BOTTOM LINE	PLAN	ACTUAL	DIFFERENCE
(Income minus Expenses)	(131)		

Harvey's SSP *After* Polishing:

SQUEEZE SPENDING PLAN (SSP) SUMMARY

Month/Yr. Master | End Date 1/28/2011 | Weeks 4

INCOME	PLAN	ACTUAL	DIFFERENCE
Income *(Take-home pay)*	3,000		
Income *(Take-home pay)*			
Other Income			
LAST MONTH - Positive Bottom Line			
TOTAL INCOME	3,000		
EXPENSES	**PLAN**	**ACTUAL**	**DIFFERENCE**
LAST MONTH - Negative Bottom Line			
(1) DEBITS / CHECKS	1,867		
(2) CASH 4 (# of weeks) x $120 (dollars/wk)	480		
(3) CREDIT CARD PAYMENTS	200		
(4) FLEXIBLE SPENDING MONEY	200		
(5) SAVINGS / INVESTMENTS	250		
TOTAL EXPENSES	2,997		
BOTTOM LINE	**PLAN**	**ACTUAL**	**DIFFERENCE**
(Income minus Expenses)	3		

CHAPTER NINE

DEVELOPING A WORKABLE MAINTENANCE PLAN

"Wealth is a result of habit"

– Unknown

"And consistently squeezing your money helps build it."

– Patricia Stallworth

Squeeze Principle #7: Including checks and balances in your spending plan allows you to self-correct and always stay in control!

Congratulations on setting up your Master *Squeeze* Spending Plan! The next step in the process is to complete the remaining parts of the form (there are two we haven't discussed yet), review it, and prepare a new plan for the coming month. Performing *Squeeze* maintenance on a monthly basis not only allows you to keep your *Squeeze Your Money* Spending Plan up-to-date, but it also provides you with the information to make good money choices.

The Four-Step Maintenance Plan

Maintaining your Monthly *Squeeze* Spending Plan (SSP) involves four basic steps that typically take less than three hours to complete. To get started, select a convenient time to perform your monthly plan maintenance. This should be a time after you receive your bank statement(s) and most of your bills so you can go through all the maintenance steps at the same time. For example, if you receive most of your bills near the end of the month, the beginning of the month might be a good time to schedule your monthly maintenance. Once you select a time, try it for a couple of months to see if it works for you.

While maintaining your plan is not a difficult process, it does require attention to detail, and interruptions can lead to mistakes so choose a time and place when you are less likely to be interrupted. Once you complete this four-step process, you're done. That's it until next month!

The four-step maintenance plan includes:

Step 1: Verify Your Account Balances (a.k.a.—Balancing Your Checkbook or Reconciliation). I know what you're thinking, but this step is important. It verifies that you have as much money in your checking account as you think you have. If you're wrong here, your next monthly spending plan could be wrong from the start, and you know what that can lead to. It's really not as bad as you think—I promise. *(P.S. – There is even a video on the website you can watch that will take you through the process step-by-step.)*

Step 2: Compare Your Planned vs. Your Actual Spending. In this step, you put in the actual dollars you spent in the column next to your PLAN amounts and calculate any difference. This will show you areas where you stayed on plan and areas were you got off track. Here again, your BOTTOM LINE number will either be positive or negative, and this number will roll forward to the next month's SSP, either leaving you with more money to spend or a shortage to make up.

Step 3: Set-Up Next Month's *Squeeze* Spending Plan. In this step, you create a plan for the coming month using the previous month as a template. Following the same steps you used in setting up your Master Spending Plan, list your income, the expenses you plan to cover, and then adjust your plan until the BOTTOM LINE is at or near zero.

Step 4: Pay Your Bills and Organize Your Paperwork. In this step, you pay the bills for the coming month and file any paperwork that you need to keep for tax purposes or that are related to open accounts.

Hey, wait a minute. That's a lot of work.

Well, let's see. Two of the four parts—balancing your checkbook and paying your bills are things you should do anyway. And, as far as completing your current spending plan and creating a new one, those are two things that will help you manage your money to meet your goals and reduce your money stress, and the whole process should take less than three hours a month. Doesn't that sound like it's worth the effort?

STEP 1: VERIFY YOUR ACCOUNT BALANCES

The purpose of this step is to determine whether there are any differences between the amount you show in your checkbook and the total your bank shows on its statement. Banks *can and do* make mistakes, but a more likely scenario is that you could make a math error or forget to include a transaction such as an ATM withdrawal that results in a difference. If any errors exist, that were either caused by you or by the bank, this is an opportunity to correct them before you plan next month's spending so you can get off to an accurate start. **Note:** There are online programs like Mint.com and software programs like Intuit's Quicken that will do a lot of the work for you, but I believe it's important to understand how the process works so you can spot when something is not right, so before you skip this part, I urge you to try working through it for at least three months, and then you can use other resources if you like.

An Overview

The main reason you and your bank may have different totals for the money in your account is because the bank's information always lags behind the updated balance in your checkbook. As long as you make transactions in your account after your bank statement's closing date, there will always be a difference.

Any amounts in your check register that are not on the bank's statement are called *outstanding items*. However, since you will be writing fewer checks and writing them earlier in the month with the *Squeeze Your Money System*, chances are you will have few, if any, outstanding items. The key to keeping the process simple is to balance your account as soon as possible after you receive your bank statement to limit the number of outstanding items.

Note: Each bank statement includes a worksheet and the steps to balance or reconcile your account. You can balance your account using your bank statement worksheet, or you can follow the steps in *"Balancing Your Checkbook 101"* on the next page, and use the *Account Balancing Worksheet* on p. 112.

If this is your first time...

If you've had a checking account for awhile but you've never balanced it before, *don't panic.* Instead of trying to start at the beginning, go back three months and start from there. Using your last three bank statements, go through your checking account register and put a checkmark in your check register next to each item that has cleared the bank. Write in differences like fees and any interest you received. Then add or subtract them from your total. Next, follow the worksheet balancing instructions (Step 5 on p. 111). List as outstanding anything that does not have a check mark next to it but was entered in your register within the last three months only. Calculate the total, and compare it to your statement total.

Balancing Your Account 101

Before you start the balancing process, gather the following items:

- your latest bank statement and your check register
- your deposit slips and receipts
- a calculator and a pencil

Balancing Your Account Steps:

1. ***Match your checks.*** Go through your bank statement's listing of checks that have cleared. Using a pen, make a checkmark in your register next to the amount of each cleared check. There's a small preprinted column next to the amount column just for this purpose. It shows a check mark at the top. (**Note:** Use different colored pens

Continued on the next page

each month in case you have to go back over your work. This makes it easy to determine which checks cleared during which month.) Don't concern yourself with the check numbers—only the amounts.

Make sure the bank amount agrees with the amount in your checkbook. If it doesn't, circle it and keep going. Don't stop until you've completed this step. Work continually from your bank statement to your check register—*never* in reverse.

2. ***List outstanding checks.*** Go back through your check register again and using the *Account Balancing Worksheet* on p. 112 or the chart on the back of your bank statement, list your outstanding checks—the checks you did not check off in your check register as having cleared the bank, as well as any outstanding debit purchases or ATM withdrawals that have not yet cleared the bank. Total the column of outstanding checks, debits, and ATM withdrawals.
3. ***Match your deposits.*** Make sure that each deposit listed on your bank statement is also recorded in your check register and that the amounts match. If you missed a deposit that is listed on your bank statement but not in your check register, add it now. Review your deposit slips and paystubs to be sure all of the deposits you made are listed. Put a checkmark next to each deposit as you did with your checks.
4. ***List your outstanding deposits.*** Go through your checkbook register and using use the *Account Balancing Worksheet* or the chart on the back of your bank

Continued on the next page

statement, list your outstanding deposits—the deposits you did not check off in your check register as having cleared the bank. Then total the column. **Note:** In bank jargon, debits take money away from your account and credits add to it.

5. ***Record interest and bank fees.*** Check your bank statement for any fees or bank charges and record them in your check register, along with any interest earned. Retotal your check register.

6. ***Record your bank statement's Ending Balance.*** Using your bank statement, record the ending balance or the total on the last day the statement covers on the Account Balancing Worksheet or chart on the back of your bank statement.

7. ***SUBTRACT the Total Checks Outstanding from the statement Ending Balance in Step 6.***

8. ***ADD the Total Deposits Outstanding to the amount calculated in Step 7.***

9. ***Celebrate!*** If the totals match, make a note in your check register next to the total to indicate you balanced to the bank statement like the word "balanced" or use your favorite symbol like ☺,★,#,☑ or ♥. On the other hand, if they don't match, check for math errors in your checkbook register such as transposed numbers (e.g., 83 instead of 38), subtracting a deposit instead of adding it, adding a check written instead of subtracting it, or automatic payments you forgot to record, etc.

Squeeze: Account Balancing Worksheet

Step 1: Match your checks

Step 2: List Outstanding Checks

Check Number/Description	Amount	
TOTAL CHECKS OUTSTANDING		

Step 3: Match your deposits

Step 4: List Outstanding Deposits

Date	Amount	
TOTAL DEPOSITS OUTSTANDING		

Step 5: Record interest and bank charges and recalculate your check register total

Step 6: Record the bank statement's ending balance ________________

Step 7: SUBTRACT the Total Checks Outstanding *(Step 6 minus Step 2)* ________________

Step 8: ADD the Total Deposits Outstanding *(Step 7 plus Step 4)* ________________

Step 9: The amount in Step 8 should match the ending balance in your check register. If it does, put a mark in your check register to indicate that it balanced. If not, an error has occurred and you may need to review the steps again.

RESOURCES & TERMS

- If balancing your checkbook is still a blur, don't worry. It will come with time. Watch the video at www.squeezeyourmoney.com. Or, if you're having trouble fixing errors, read the article, "Tips and Strategies to Find and Fix Errors When Balancing Your Checkbook" also located on the *Squeeze* website.

- www.Quicken.com - www.Mint.com

STEP 2: COMPARE YOUR PLANNED VS. YOUR ACTUAL SPENDING

In this step, you put in the actual dollars you spent and compare them to your plan. This is important because it provides the necessary feedback (either positive or negative) to start next month's SSP with accurate Bottom Line information, and it helps provide the motivation to stay on track or improve next month.

Getting Started

Start the process by listing all of your checkbook entries that apply to the past month on your past month's SSP *Debit/Check Worksheet* in the column labeled ACTUAL. As you do this, mark the entry in your checkbook with the first letter of the month it belongs to with a colored pen. (**Note:** Use a different color pen for each month. For example, mark January entries in blue and February in red. As you go through your checkbook, enter all unmarked new items on the appropriate SSP Worksheet (Debit/Checks, Cash, Credit Card Payments, Flexible Spending Money, or Savings) for the month completed unless they are recent and apply to the upcoming month. Then enter the totals on the appropriate line on your SSP in the ACTUAL column.)

Once you've entered all of the numbers on your SSP, add your TOTAL EXPENSES and deduct this from your TOTAL INCOME. This is your ACTUAL BOTTOM LINE for the month and it should match the amount in your account(s).

How did you do? Is your BOTTOM LINE better, right on target, or worse than you planned? If it is more than a little off either way, meaning you spent more or less than you planned, look at each of the categories in question and compare the total you *actually* spent with the amount you *planned* to spend and calculate the difference. Place this amount in the DIFFERENCE column. If the difference is favorable (you received more income or you spent *less* than you planned), put a plus (+) sign next to it. If it's unfavorable (you received less income or you spent more than you planned), put a minus (-) sign next to it. This way, you can see at a glance what you need to focus your attention on for next month's SSP.

Don't be discouraged if you see more minus signs than plus signs. It's possible that you will not match your SSP the first few times you do it. Remember, you are learning a new skill, so be patient with yourself. When you overspend despite your best efforts to follow your SSP, think about what might have happened if you didn't have a plan and you weren't *trying* to manage your spending.

Use the feedback from the ACTUAL column to make appropriate changes to next month's SSP so it is attainable. When you look over your DIFFERENCE column, ask yourself how you will handle these areas next month? Do you need to do a better job with your spending? Or do you need to make modest changes in your lifestyle or possibly even major ones such as taking in a roommate or downsizing to a less expensive home or car? Can you increase your income? If so, how soon can you make that happen? Take a moment to reflect on the information you've just gained and the changes you want to make. Then decide on a plan for the coming month that reflects all of the ideas you have. The main purpose is for your spending to fit you and, ultimately, help you achieve your goals.

STEP 2: RECAP

1. Using your check register and receipts, enter the actual amounts you spent in each category on the appropriate SSP worksheet (e.g., Debit/Checks, Cash, Credit Card Payments, Flexible Spending Money, and Savings). Then enter the totals on your Monthly SSP in the column titled ACTUAL next to the appropriate category.
2. Calculate the difference between your planned and actual and place that number in the column titled DIFFERENCE. If the difference is favorable, place a plus (+) sign next to it. It's unfavorable (your income was less than expected or you spent more than your PLAN number, place a minus sign (-) next to it.

(***Note:*** *See Harvey's completed plan on the next page.*)

Harvey's completed plan:

SQUEEZE SPENDING PLAN (SSP) SUMMARY

Month/Yr. Master | End Date 1/28/2011 | Weeks 4

INCOME	PLAN	ACTUAL	DIFFERENCE
Income *(Take-home pay)*	3,000	3,000	0
Income *(Take-home pay)*			
Other Income			
LAST MONTH - Positive Bottom Line			
TOTAL INCOME	3,000	3,000	0
EXPENSES	**PLAN**	**ACTUAL**	**DIFFERENCE**
LAST MONTH - Negative Bottom Line			
(1) DEBITS / CHECKS	1,867	1,867	0
(2) CASH 4 (# of weeks) x $120 (dollars/wk)	480	520	(40) -
(3) CREDIT CARD PAYMENTS	200	200	0
(4) FLEXIBLE SPENDING MONEY	200	295	(95) -
(5) SAVINGS / INVESTMENTS	250	250	0
TOTAL EXPENSES	2,997	3,132	(135)
BOTTOM LINE	**PLAN**	**ACTUAL**	**DIFFERENCE**
(Income minus Expenses)	3	(132)	(129)

STEP 3: CREATE A NEW SPENDING PLAN

This is your opportunity to get off to a fresh start—to take the information you gained from your spending last month and develop a new plan for the coming month that is workable for you. So strategize, play with the numbers, manipulate your money on paper, and explore your options. If you're making great progress toward your goals, it's going to show up right there in black and white. However, if you're not satisfied with your progress, this is your opportunity to recommit to your financial goals and develop new plans, schemes, and action items to move forward. Your Monthly SSP is your tool to turn your dreams and ideas into reality.

Unless you want or need to make additional changes, the only real change you will need to make from your Master SSP is to replace your estimates with the actual amounts of your bills and expenses. For example, when you were developing your Master SSP, you estimated the amount of your bills for utilities. Now you can enter the exact amount in each category directly from the bills. Also, on your Master SSP, you may have allowed 10 percent of your income for Flexible Spending Money. When you prepare your new Monthly SSP, review your calendar and notes and make a list of the specific one-time expenses you know about for the coming month. Then list them on your Flexible Spending Money Worksheet. With exact dollar amounts, you can see exactly how much money you will need to cover your expenses, how much money you will have available, how much debt you can pay off, and how much you can put into savings.

Completing Your New Monthly SSP

To complete this task you will need a new SSP form and worksheets as well as your paystubs, bills, statements, etc.

Enter the End Date and Number of Weeks in the month (four or five) on the SSP form. Next enter your income, including your salary and any additional income for the month in the INCOME section and enter the total in the TOTAL INCOME PLAN column.

Next, take a look at the previous month's BOTTOM LINE and transfer that amount to the new SSP. If the bottom line is positive, transfer the amount to the line titled LAST MONTH—Positive Bottom Line in the INCOME section of the SSP. This will add to the amount of money you have available for the coming month. On the other, hand if it is a negative amount, transfer it to the line titled LAST MONTH—Negative Bottom Line in the EXPENSE section of the SSP. This will decrease the amount of money you have available for the coming month. In essence, you've borrowed from the coming month to pay for last month's expenses.

DON'T FORGET TO TRANSFER THE PREVIOUS MONTH'S BOTTOM LINE (POSITIVE OR NEGATIVE) TO THE NEW SSP.

Finally, using your Master SSP worksheets or last month's SSP worksheets as a guide, complete your SSP worksheets and enter the totals on the main SSP form in the column titled PLAN:

(1) **Debit/Check Worksheet** — Using your actual bills, enter the amounts on the worksheet, total them for the month, and enter the total on the SSP form in the DEBITS/CHECKS PLAN column.

(2) **Cash Worksheet** – Review last month's worksheet and if nothing major has changed, go directly to the SSP form to the CASH line and enter the number of weeks (either four or five), and your weekly cash amount. Then multiply the two together and enter the total in the CASH PLAN column.

(3) **Credit Card Payments Worksheet** – Review your card statements, enter the balance, interest rate, due date, and minimum payment. Then list the amount you plan to pay for the coming month. Add up the amounts you plan to pay and enter the total on your SSP form next to CREDIT CARD PAYMENTS in the PLAN column.

(4) **Flexible Spending Money Worksheet** – Review your annual calendar and list any expenses you know will be coming up in the month such as birthdays or car repairs, etc. Then review last month's SSP to see if you had any expenses that were not paid off such as a doctor's visit. Next check your "Wish List" to see if there is a must-have purchase for this month, and finally add some money for spontaneous spending (dinner out with friends, etc.). Total all of these on your worksheet. Then enter the total on your SSP in the FLEXIBLE SPENDING MONEY PLAN column.

(5) **Savings/Investment Worksheet** – Review your goals from last month, and make any necessary changes in the goal(s) or amount(s). Then carry that total over to your SSP form, and enter it in the SAVINGS/INVESTMENTS PLAN column. (**Note:** If you haven't reached your emergency fund goal or if you had to dip into it, remember to add to or

replenish it.)

Once you complete all of the worksheets and enter the total on the SSP Summary Form, add all of the EXPENSES and enter the total on the line titled TOTAL EXPENSES.

Finally, calculate your planned BOTTOM LINE—Subtract your TOTAL EXPENSES from your TOTAL Income. If the number is positive, decide where you want to spend the extra money, and if it's negative, keep working on it until it is zero. Read Chapter 8 for more information on spending cuts. (***Note:*** *See Harvey's plan for next month on the next page.)*

Hey, wait a minute. What if I get some extra money, like $1,000 or even $10,000? How should I put that in my spending plan?

Good question, Harvey. If you get some extra money, whether you win it, sell something, or you get it in some other way, you can use it in several ways. You can always use it to pay bills or add to your savings, but also consider spending a portion of it, at least ten percent, on something you enjoy—something that you will remember.

On the other hand, if this is a pay raise—something that you can depend on month after month—avoid changing your lifestyle or going on a buying spree. Instead, celebrate once and then use the extra money each month either to pay down your debts or add to your savings based on your goals.

Harvey's plan for next month:

SQUEEZE SPENDING PLAN (SSP) SUMMARY

Month/Yr. February-11   End Date 2/25/2011   Weeks 4

INCOME	PLAN	ACTUAL	DIFFERENCE
Income *(Take-home pay)*	2,700		
Income *(Take-home pay)*			
Other Income			
LAST MONTH - Positive Bottom Line →			
TOTAL INCOME	2,700		
EXPENSES	**PLAN**	**ACTUAL**	**DIFFERENCE**
LAST MONTH - Negative Bottom Line →	129		
(1) DEBITS / CHECKS	1,861		
(2) CASH 4 (# of weeks) x $120 (dollars/wk)	480		
(3) CREDIT CARD PAYMENTS	100		
(4) FLEXIBLE SPENDING MONEY	130		
(5) SAVINGS / INVESTMENTS	0		
TOTAL EXPENSES	2,700		
BOTTOM LINE	**PLAN**	**ACTUAL**	**DIFFERENCE**
(Income minus Expenses)	0		

Next month is going to be a very tight month for Harvey. He not only has less money available, but he went over the amount he planned to spend this month and that added to his expenses for next month. *(See Last Month – Negative Bottom Line p. 116)* He's not happy with a zero Savings amount for the coming month and he is actively looking for ways to generate additional income.

STEP 4: PAY YOUR BILLS AND ORGANIZE YOUR PAPERWORK

There's nothing particularly difficult or complicated about paying bills, but it does help if you develop a system you follow each month. Since you've already completed your spending plan for the month, you know exactly what you're going to pay, so the process should be very straightforward. Your goal with this last step is to simply get the paperwork finished quickly and correctly. And you can make this process go even more quickly if you automate a large portion of the process.

Here's the system I use. Feel free to modify it anyway you like. Or if you already have a system that's working for you, continue to follow it. The important thing is that you have an organized system to follow each month.

Sample Bill-Paying System:

- As bills or any money related items such bank statements, deposit slips, and receipts come in, place them in a central location. If you receive bill statements online, print a copy and keep it with your bills. I like to drop mine in a basket where I also keep a calculator, pens, stamps, and everything I need to pay bills, but you could also use a drawer, a filing cabinet, or even a shoebox. It doesn't matter as long as it's convenient and large enough for you keep everything together. (**Note:** At the end of the month everything will be cleaned out in preparation for the next month.)
- Review each bill, check to be sure that the amounts are correct and that you have received credit for last month's

payment, and then circle the due date and the amount due.

- Create a bill for any expenses you pay each month but do not receive a bill for, such as church or charity, and place it with your bills to serve as a reminder. Create it once and then keep re-using it.
- Once a month pay your all of bills at once either by check or online. Don't forget about bills that you have scheduled for automatic withdrawal.

File any paperwork you need for tax purposes, open accounts, or warranties. In general, keep regular bill statements until the payment shows up on the next statement and keep general receipts for at least six months in case you need to return or repair an item. *For more information on what to keep and how long to keep it, see p. 147.*

Hey, wait a minute. What if I can't afford to pay all of my bills at once because I get paid twice a month?

No problem. If you mail your bills, prepare them as usual and put a sticky note on the envelope with the amount and the date to mail it so it will be on time. Or, if you pay your bills online, circle the amount and the due date and place them in order with the earliest due date on top and clip them together. Then as money comes in, mail or pay any of the remaining bills you clipped together.

Automate as Much of the Process as Possible

There are some parts of the process that you can automate, and doing so will not only save you time but lots of headaches and missed opportunities. Once you have had an opportunity to use the *Squeeze* Spending Plan for a few months, you will begin to see patterns emerging—patterns related to how much you need to pay your bills, how much you can generally put in Savings/Investments and how much you need for Flexible Spending Money. Then you can set up automatic transfers to those accounts directly from the account where you deposit your paycheck. And, if changes are necessary, you can always make manual transfers. The diagram on the next page shows one example of how you could set up your accounts to *squeeze* the most out of every dollar.

The key point in *Step 1* of the diagram above is to direct deposit your paycheck to a checking, savings, or *high-yield savings* account. If you choose to deposit your check into a high yield savings account, you will generally earn a higher rate of interest, and this can be a plus, especially if you have money left over each month or you keep the majority of your cash cushion there.

In *Step 2*, set up automatic transfers to your bill-paying account and your savings/investment accounts.

Finally, in *Step 3*, set up automatic transfers between your bill-paying checking account and other accounts such as your Flexible Spending Money account and any special accounts for bills you pay less frequently than monthly so you can transfer funds back and forth as needed.

Link Your Accounts to Simplify Automation

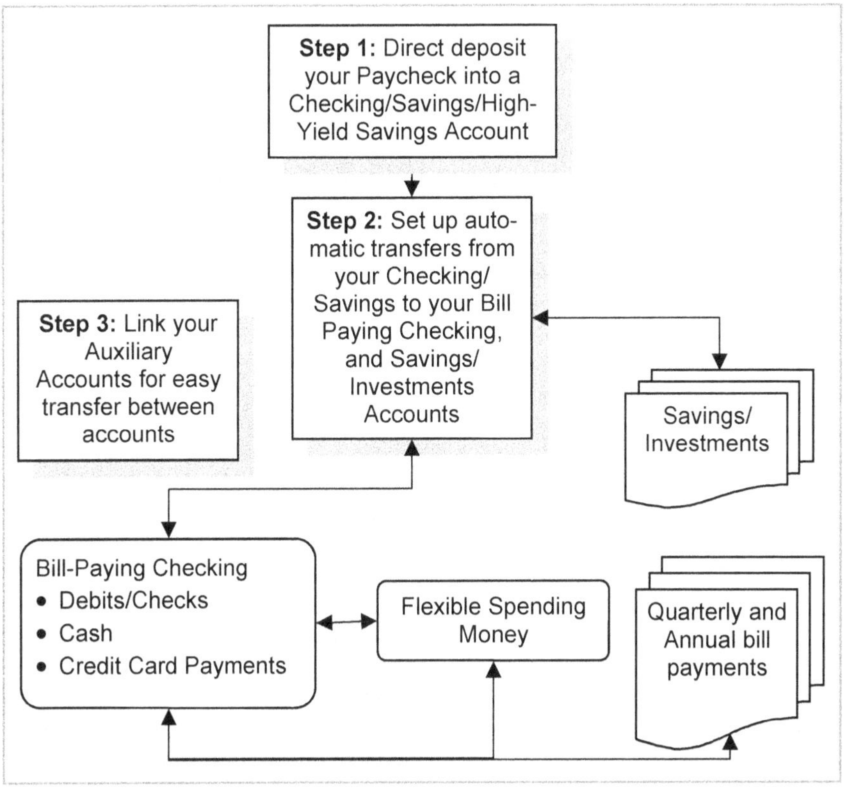

Step 1: Direct deposit your Paycheck into a Checking/Savings/High-Yield Savings Account

Step 2: Set up automatic transfers from your Checking/ Savings to your Bill Paying Checking, and Savings/ Investments Accounts

Step 3: Link your Auxiliary Accounts for easy transfer between accounts

Savings/ Investments

Bill-Paying Checking
- Debits/Checks
- Cash
- Credit Card Payments

Flexible Spending Money

Quarterly and Annual bill payments

There are lots of ways to configure your accounts, and this is just one example. The key is to have a clear idea of what you need to keep monthly in each account and that comes from keeping your *Squeeze* Spending Plan up-to-date.

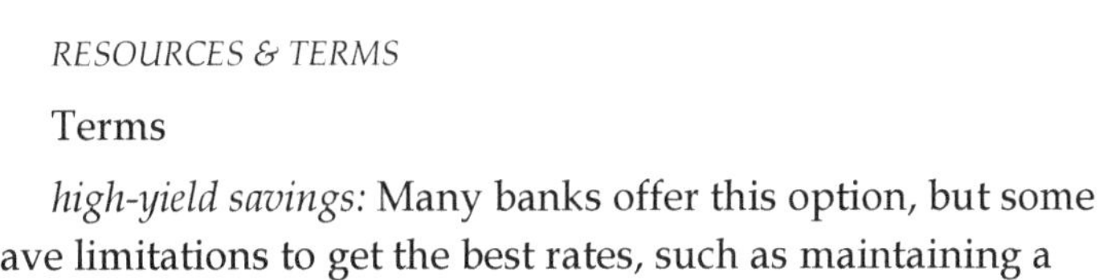

RESOURCES & TERMS

Terms

high-yield savings: Many banks offer this option, but some also have limitations to get the best rates, such as maintaining a

Continued on the next page

RESOURCES & TERMS (continued)

balance of $25,000 or more. However, there are a few banks that don't, and these are generally online banks like ING Direct (www.ingdirect.com) and Ally (www.ally.com). Another place to look for competitive rates is at Bankrate.com. Be sure to check out all of your options as the rates will vary widely.

Hey, wait a minute. I'm not sure what should I do about bills that I only pay annually or quarterly like my estimated taxes?

Good question, Harvey. One of the best ways to handle bills that you pay less often than monthly is to set aside a portion of the bill each month in a separate account so that when the bill arrives, you have the money to pay it. For example, if you have a $600 insurance bill that is due annually, divide the total amount by 12 and set aside $50 each month to pay the bill. If you set up your accounts like the diagram on the previous page, you can setup an automatic transfer each month from your main checking account and forget about it.

Basic Benefits of the *Squeeze* Spending Plan

Well, that's it. You have the whole *Squeeze* Spending Plan process, and this is a good place to stop to consider the benefits, and recommit to working on your plan on a monthly basis. Here are three basic benefits of *Squeeze*.

First, it reduces your money-related stress. Because you

get to spend your money on paper before you do so in real life, you get the benefit of foresight, and you can avoid many problems before they occur. For example, if you generally worry about running out of money throughout the month, you can use the information from your SSP to plan and communicate that information to the people who need it, i.e., your creditors, family members, people who depend on your support, and most importantly to yourself. Once you finalize your Monthly SSP, all you need to do is follow it. Further worrying is not necessary—it's all there in black and white, and if negative thoughts creep in throughout the month, you can simply remind yourself how committed you are to following your SSP and improving your situation.

BECAUSE YOU GET TO SPEND YOUR MONEY ON PAPER BEFORE YOU DO SO IN REAL LIFE, YOU GET THE BENEFIT OF FORESIGHT AND YOU CAN AVOID MANY PROBLEMS BEFORE THEY

Second, the process provides you with accurate information to make the changes necessary to reach your financial goals. Each month you have the opportunity to review your situation and make decisions about what to do. Being on track can make you feel good about situation and your money. And, when you're not, you have the information and tools you need to make immediate changes.

Third, are the subtle changes that can occur in your spending behavior over time as you begin to focus on your plan. Don't be surprised if you are off track the first few months or even for the first year. But after that, if you genuinely believe in the spending decisions you make on your SSP and you want to make them a reality, your spending behavior will gradually change to accommodate your plan. So it is extremely important that you that you stick with the program and continue to work on completing your SSP each month, even when you get off track. As I said earlier, this is a marathon, not a sprint, and you have time to correct your course, so be patient with yourself. And never stop *Squeezing*!

SQUEEZE POINTS:

- ***Squeeze Principle #7: Including checks and balances in your spending plan allows you to self-correct and always stay in control!***
- There are four steps in maintaining your plan: verifying your account balances; comparing your planned income and expenses to your actual ones; setting up a new *Squeeze* plan for the coming month; and paying your bills. All of these together should take no more than three hours a month to complete.
- When completing your *Squeeze* plan for the coming month, don't forget to add or subtract the BOTTOM LINE balance from the previous month before you calculate your total income and expenses for the current month. If you spent less than you planned, you will have more money available for the coming month. And if you spent more than you planned, you will have less for the coming month. (**Note:** See Harvey's current and new plan on pages 116 and 121.)

SQUEEZE POINTS *(continued)*:

- Look for ways to make the process as smooth as possible, like having a set time each month for *Squeeze* maintenance, developing a bill-paying system, and automating transfers between your various accounts.

SQUEEZE ACTION ITEMS:

1. Schedule a time to maintain and update your spending plan. The best time is when you can perform a number of maintenance tasks at once, such as balancing your bank account and paying your bills. If you receive most of your statements and bills near the end of the month, the beginning of the month might be a good time.
2. Once you create a monthly plan, go through all four steps in the maintenance process:
   a. Verifying your account balances
   b. Updating your current SSP with ACTUAL numbers.
   c. Completing a new SSP for the coming month.
   d. Paying bills and organizing your paperwork

   Some supplies you will need to complete these exercises include the following:

   - your latest bank statement, check register, deposit slips and receipts

Continued on the next page

SQUEEZE **ACTION ITEMS:** *(continued)*

- a basket, drawer, or shoebox to store incoming bills and financial documents
- a copy of your current SSP and worksheets
- your bank account balancing worksheet or a copy of the Account Balancing Worksheet in this chapter, a new SSP Summary form and the worksheets to complete the SSP form. All are available at www.squeezeyourmoney.com
- an accordion file, file drawer or box to store the documents you keep
- a calculator
- a shredder
- folders, envelopes, and labels to organize and file your expenses and financial documents
- colored pencils, and/or pens

3. Research high-yield savings account options online and at brick-and-mortar banks. Ask about rates, minimum balances, fees, and account transfer options. Then, using the example on p. 125, develop a plan and a flow chart for your accounts so you have a visual reminder of how it all works.

PART 3

CHAPTER TEN

SQUEEZE ACTION STRATEGIES

"Prosperity is a way of living and thinking, and not just money or things. Poverty is a way of living and thinking, and not just a lack of money or things."
— Eric Butterworth

"The real difference between these two is attitude and action."
— Patricia Stallworth

You Have a Spending Plan. Now What?

Because you have a life beyond your spending plan, *Squeeze* Action Strategies were designed to give you the same kind of control you have with the *Squeeze* Spending Plan (SSP), but on a much broader scale, for the remaining parts of your financial life.

"...YOUR $PENDING PLAN AND ACTION $TRATEGIE$ FORM A CONTINUOU$ LOOP WITH EACH ONE INFLUENCING THE OTHER."

Squeeze Action Strategies (SAS) not only pick up where your spending plan leaves off, but together they form a continuous loop, with each one influencing the other. Every month when you complete your spending plan, you have the opportunity for a fresh start and your actions during the month create a better (or worse) ending to start the next month. Then the cycle repeats each month.

The Real Purpose of SAS

Your actions are powerful. They determine your income, the bills you must pay, and the amount of money available to fund your goals. The real purpose of *Squeeze* Action Strategies (SAS) is to channel your actions in ways that move you closer to your goals by allowing you to see everything on paper, much like you did with your spending plan, before you take any actions. In other words, SAS provides you with options—options to determine the outcomes you want and options to *squeeze* even more out of your dollars.

How to Use SAS to Manage the Rest of Your Financial Life

Squeeze Action Strategies (SAS) focus on five basic areas as well as cash management information from your spending plan. Together they make up the essential planning areas of your financial life *(see the diagram on the next page)*. The remaining five areas include:

1. Tracking your stuff and stats (the things you own and owe) so you always know where you are financially. *(Chapter 11)*

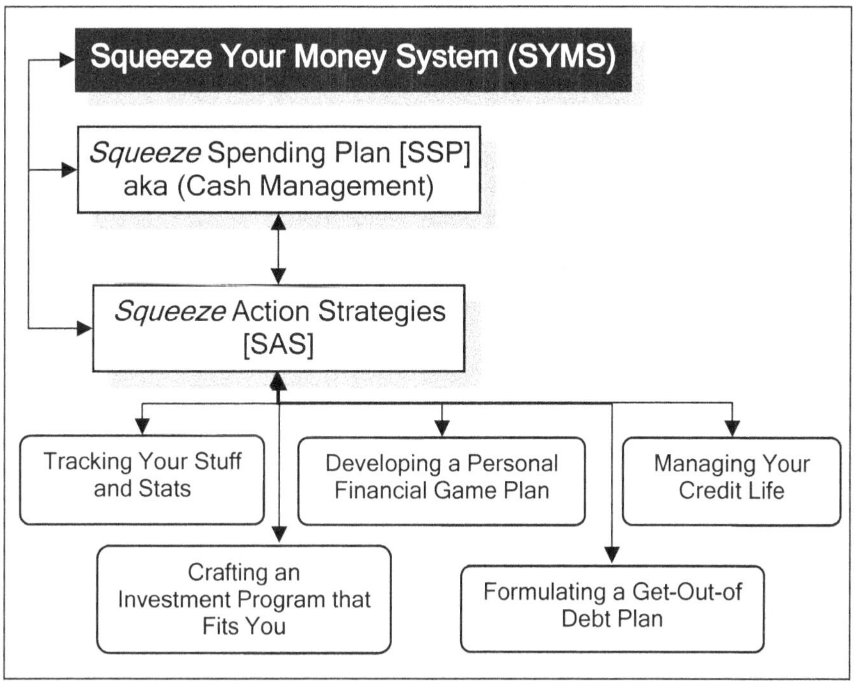

2. Developing a personal financial game plan to serve as a guide to get you where you want to go. *(Chapter 12)*
3. Crafting a personal investment program that fits you and your goals. *(Chapter 13)*
4. Managing your credit life to keep your records accurate and working for you. *(Chapter 14)*
5. Formulating a get-out and stay-out-of-debt plan so all your extra dollars go to places you want them to. *(Chapter 15)*

We will cover the essentials in each of these key areas in the next five chapters. However, there's a lot more flexibility in completing the SAS than with the spending plan, and you can focus less attention on those areas that don't relate to you. For example, if debt is not an issue or concern of yours, you can skip Chapter 15 altogether. And if you already have an investment program in place, chances are you can just scan Chapter 13 to be sure you understand the basics. If, at any time, you want more than the essentials in these key areas, you can build on the foundation here by using other resources or another book in the *Squeeze Your Money* series.

(Note: Visit www.squeezeyourmoney.com *for more information about current and upcoming books in the Squeeze Your Money series.)*

SQUEEZE POINTS:

- The *Squeeze* Spending Plan (SSP) and the *Squeeze* Action Strategies (SAS) work together so you can manage all of the essential areas of your financial life.
- Unlike SSP, each of the key areas of SAS can work independently so you can focus less attention on the areas that are less important to you.

SQUEEZE ACTION ITEMS:

In preparation for the next chapters, print out your last SSP Summary and background worksheets.

CHAPTER ELEVEN

TRACKING YOUR STUFF AND STATS

"Money is only a tool. It will take you wherever you wish, but it will not replace you as the driver."

– Ayn Rand

"So go ahead, take the wheel."

– Patricia Stallworth

Squeeze Principle #8: Knowing what you own and what you owe is essential before you add to either list!

It's tough to make good money decisions if you don't know your current financial situation. This chapter focuses on compiling and tracking your financial information as well as calculating some important money stats so you are better prepared when opportunities or challenges come your way.

Key Benefits of Knowing Where You Are at All Times

Knowing where you are at all times financially has four key benefits: (1) it greatly simplifies the process of decision making because you have the information to understand the implications and consequences of different choices; (2) it's a form of keeping score so you always know how close you are to achieving your goals; (3) it allows you to spot potential problems and do something about them before they become major obstacles; and (4) it gives you the chance to evaluate opportunities that come your way so you can determine how they will fit with what you already have. There are several indicators that can help you track where you are at all times and we will explore four important areas to watch in this chapter.

Important Stuff and Stats to Track

Major indicators you can use to track where you are at all times include your *cash management* or spending plan; your *assets* (things you own like personal investments); your *liabilities* (things you owe like loans); and the estate and risk planning strategies you have in place. And before you can determine how to *squeeze* the most out of these, you must first have a clear picture of where you are in each area.

AREAS TO WATCH: YOUR CASH FLOW, ASSETS, LIABILITIES, AND ESTATE AND RISK PLANNING.

CASH MANAGEMENT

Your cash management or spending plan determines your cash flow, and it is important because it forms the foundation for the type of actions you can take. In other words, how you manage your money not only determines how much money you have available to meet your needs today, but how much discretionary money you have for savings and investments for your future.

If you completed the *Squeeze* Spending Plan series *(Chapters 2 – 9)* you already have a good idea of your basic cash flow numbers, such as how much you spend in each of the major categories (debits/checks, cash, credit card payments, savings/investments, etc.). However, it's also important to understand what percent of your income goes towards paying off your expenses and what percent goes toward savings. This is important because if your expenses are too high it will show up in decreased savings. Two important measures relating to cash management are the debt-to-income ratio and the savings ratio.

The Debt-to-Income Ratio

The debt-to-income ratio (DTI) represents the percent of your income that goes toward paying debts, and the lower the number the better. DTI can be calculated in two different ways:

1. **The front-end DTI ratio** indicates the percent of your income that goes toward housing costs. For renters this is the rent amount and for homeowners this includes all payments associated with the house—mortgage payments, insurance premiums, property taxes, and homeowners' association dues divided by your gross income. In general, lenders recommend a front-end ratio of 28 percent or less *(see the sample on the next page).*

2. **The back-end DTI ratio** indicates the percent of income that goes toward paying all recurring debt payments, including those covered by the front-end DTI as well as other debts, such as credit cards, car payments, student loan payments, child support,

alimony, etc. In general, lenders recommend a back-end ratio of 36 percent or less.

Here's an example of how to calculate the debt-to-income ratio:

Charles has a monthly gross income *(the amount he earns before paying taxes or anything else)* of $4,000. His total housing costs are $1,200 and his total monthly debt, including his housing costs are $1,700.

Squeeze: Debt-to-Income Worksheet

SOURCE	AMOUNT	EXPENSES ÷ INCOME	DEBT-TO-INCOME RATIOS
Monthly Gross Income	$4,000		
Monthly Housing Costs	$1,200	1200 ÷ 4000	Front-end DTI = 30%
Monthly Total Debt Payments	$1,700	1700 ÷ 4000	Back-end DTI = 43%

Note: The two forms of DTI are often expressed as a pair such as 30/43. Also, Charles's back-end DTI is high compared to the recommended percent, and that indicates his total debt is high for the level of income he has. To correct this, he should look for ways to increase his income or decrease his debt.

Now it's your turn. Using information from your SSP and the worksheet on the next page, calculate your front-end and back-end DTI. How did you do? If your ratios are a lot higher than the recommended numbers, look for ways to lower them. For example, if your front-end DTI is above 30 percent, it's a signal that your housing costs are too high for your current income level. Look for ways to increase your income or cut your housing expenses. Or, if your front-end DTI is okay but your back-end DTI is high (above 40 percent), it's a signal that your loans and/or credit cards are taking up too much of your income, and you could possibly benefit from a debt-reduction plan like the one outlined in Chapter 15. Deciding whether or not you have too much debt is often a tough call, especially if you have the money to pay your bills, but remember there's a lot more to life than just paying bills, and if that's all you're able to do, you're missing out on a lot.

Squeeze: Debt-to-Income Worksheet

Instructions: Using the information from your *Squeeze* Spending Plan, calculate your front-end and back-end DTI.

SOURCE	AMOUNT	EXPENSES ÷ INCOME	DEBT-TO-INCOME RATIOS
Monthly Gross Income			
Monthly Housing Costs			Front-end DTI =
Monthly Total Debt Payments			Back-end DTI =

The Savings Ratio

What percent of your *gross income* are you saving? Knowing what you're currently saving is an important part of making sure that you'll achieve your financial goals. The savings ratio compares the amount of your monthly savings to your monthly income. This includes the amount you currently set aside in Savings/Investments plus any dollars that may be deducted through payroll deductions. If you have a savings goal, this is a good way to see if you're on track.

Savings Ratio Example: Barbara has a *gross income* of $2,800. She has $200 deducted from your paycheck for retirement and she sets aside $100 in her spending plan, so her total savings are $300, and a saving ratio of almost 11 percent.

	Total Savings	Gross Income	Savings ÷ Income
Barbara	$300	$2,800	.107 or 11%
Yours			

What percent of your income are you saving? In the space above, calculate your savings ratio. How did you do?

MORE IMPORTANT STUFF TO TRACK

Your cash management information is one important area to watch, and some others include your assets, liabilities, and estate and risk-planning strategies. One of the best ways to review this information is by compiling a detailed record of each area. Use the *Squeeze* Financial Inventory (see Appendix A). Download a copy from the *Squeeze* website (www.squeezeyourmoney.com) or use a similar program. The important thing is to assemble this information in a format that is easily accessible so you can evaluate each part. Once you collect this information you will have the data you need to complete a *net-worth statement (a financial snapshot of your current situation)* and essential parts of a financial roadmap *(Chapter (12)*.

ASSETS *(things you own)*

Compile information in three areas: personal investments, retirement accounts, and real estate.

- *Personal Investments*

  Personal investments include accounts you have with banks, credit unions, mutual fund companies and brokerage houses, as well as equity in a business. Typical categories include cash (checking, savings, and money market) accounts which are available at any time, as well as longer-term investments like stocks, bonds, and mutual funds.

- *Retirement Accounts*

  This includes both employer-sponsored accounts like 401(k) s and 403(b)s and personal IRAs.

- *Real Estate*

  This includes property you own, including your personal residence and any income property.

LIABILITIES *(things you owe)*

This includes credit card debt, student loans, personal loans, car or boat loans and all other personal debt.

ESTATE AND RISK-PLANNING STRATEGIES

This includes personal documents such as a will or trust, power of attorney, insurance policies, and tax-planning information.

Hey, wait a minute. I don't make a lot of money, and I'm really young. Why do I need to be concerned with tracking estate-planning stuff?

Good question, Harvey. Some estate planning "stuff" is important regardless of your age or income. Here are three

Continued on the next page

Harvey's Question *(continued)*

important estate planning documents everyone needs:

1. **A durable power of attorney** to authorize someone to act on your behalf in the event that you become physically or mentally incapacitated.
2. **A living will** that makes your wishes known regarding life prolonging medical treatments. It may also be referred to as an advance-, health care-, or physician's- directive.
3. **A will** to let people know what to do with your "stuff" and who you would like to be the guardian of any minor children you have. Failing to appoint a guardian leaves this decision up to the state in the event of your death.

What's Your *Net* Worth?

Basically, your net worth consists of everything you own (assets) minus everything you owe (liabilities). And a net-worth statement summarizes all of your relevant financial information and provides you with an instant snapshot of your financial condition at a given point in time. Knowing your net worth is especially helpful in making major financial decisions, such as deciding whether you can handle additional debt to finance large purchases. In fact, most lenders require you to complete applications that are, in essence, net-worth statements combined with some income information.

Net worth statements are also useful for deciding how to allocate your investment assets. All businesses, regardless of their size, use a form of a net worth statements or balance sheets. Even though they are different in some ways, the concepts on which they're based are essentially the same, so understanding net worth statements will not only help you manage your personal finances better, but also enhance your ability to understand business statements as you research companies to invest in.

While each net worth statement represents a snapshot at a specific point in time, in between snapshots your life is like a moving picture. You are earning and spending money, buying assets and selling them, incurring new debt and paying down your liabilities. So it's a good idea to take snapshots of your finances at least annually, or more often depending on your goals, to keep track of your progress. To track your progress, compare your net worth from two different points in time such as your current net worth with your net worth last year. Evaluating the changes in your net worth shows you how your finances are doing overall. Increases in your net worth are always a good indicator that your wealth base is increasing, so this makes it an important number to watch.

THE HIGHER YOUR NET WORTH, THE MORE LIKELY YOU ARE TO BE ABLE TO SURVIVE LIFE'S FINANICAL DIFFICULTIES.

The higher your net worth, the more likely you are to be able to survive life's financial difficulties—unemployment, financial losses, etc. because you can most likely use your assets to obtain the cash needed to deal with a financial emergency by either using them as collateral for a loan or by selling the them for cash. Net worth is an accepted measure of financial health because it quantifies the amount of cushion available to cover your financial needs.

The basic formula for a net-worth statement is:

Net Worth = Assets - Liabilities

Assets include cash on hand—checking accounts, savings, certificates of deposit (CDs), stocks, bonds, mutual funds, your house and cars, the cash value of life insurance policies, retirement plans, annuities, real estate and business interests, household furnishings, antiques, jewelry, coins, and artwork. In other words, assets are anything of value you own that could be sold. When estimating the value of your assets, don't worry if you don't have the exact dollar amounts. Simply write down the amount you think you could reasonably sell each item for today or its *fair market value*.

Liabilities include outstanding loans (student, auto, installment), mortgages, credit cards, unpaid bills (medical, utilities, etc.), and taxes you owe (income tax, real estate taxes, etc.).

Once you have a complete listing of all of your assets and liabilities, you simply subtract your liabilities from your assets to get your net worth. If you have more assets than liabilities, you will have a positive net worth, and that's a good thing. It means that you have a good base to start with. If, on the other hand, your liabilities are greater than your assets, you will have a negative net worth, and while that's not the best thing, it's important to know so that you can determine areas you need to work on to grow your net worth and your wealth.

Common ways to increase your net worth include increasing your savings, increasing the return on your investments, decreasing your debt, or a combination of these, so look for ways to incorporate these strategies into your overall financial plan. So to keep moving forward, set a goal to increase your net worth by a specific dollar amount or percentage in the next year. Remember, conducting a net worth analysis each year not only points out where you are but it gives you a consistent way to track your wealth as it grows.

Calculating Your Net Worth

Calculating your net worth may look like a difficult task but it's not so hard once you know the basics. Take the case of Sarah Jones. On December 31, she had $300 in cash, $2,700 in her checking account, and a car that she bought for $14,000. Sarah owes $6,900 on the car loan and $8,000 in student loans. *(See Sarah's net worth statement below.)*

Statement of Net Worth December 31, 2010

ASSETS		LIABILITIES	
Cash	$ 300	Car loan	$ 6,900
Checking account	2,700	Student loan	8,000
Car	14,000		
Total Assets	$17,000	Total Liabilities	$14,900

NET WORTH = $17,000 - $14,900 = $2,100

Note: Net worth statements may be formatted with assets and liabilities side by side like Sarah's example above or in a single column like the example on the next page.

Instructions: Place the totals from the *Financial Inventory Worksheet (see Appendix A)* in the appropriate categories. Total each section and then subtract your assets from your liabilities to calculate your net worth. Next project an amount or percent to increase your net worth in one, three, and seven years.

STATEMENT OF NET WORTH ____________
Date

Assets

Total Cash $ ____________
Total Fixed Income $ ____________
Total Stocks $ ____________
Total Mutual Funds $ ____________
Total Annuities $ ____________
Total Other Assets $ ____________
Total Retirement Accounts $ ____________
Total Real Estate $ ____________
Total Assets $ ____________

Liabilities

Total Mortgages $ ____________
Total Car/Boat Loans$ ____________
Total Credit Card Debt $ ____________
Total Student Loans $ ____________
Total Personal Loans$ ____________
Total All Other Debt $ ____________
Total Liabilities $ ____________

Net Worth

Total Assets $ ____________
– Total Liabilities – $ ____________
Estimated Net Worth $ ____________

Goal for Net Worth in:

1-Year ________ 3-Years _________ 7-Years _________

Signed: ____________________________ Date:____________

Signed: ____________________________

Organizing Your Financial Papers

If you haven't already done so, this is a great time to organize your financial papers because you will need many of them to complete your *Squeeze Financial Inventory*. It's so much easier to keep up with where you are if you know where everything is. Here are some tips on what to keep and what you can toss.

Now that the Internal Revenue Service (IRS) is accepting electronic records, organizing is a lot easier because there's less paper to organize. Instead of holding onto every paper, you can scan receipts and download documents from many websites as needed. However, before you start tossing, check your financial institutions policies to see how long you will have access to your statements and records. For example, some banks and credit card companies will have your statements available online for as long as seven years, and that's typically long enough in most instances if you are audited by the IRS. If that's true in your case, you can shred a lot of documents instead of holding onto them.

Stuff to Keep Indefinitely

There are certain documents, though, that should be kept indefinitely or for a long period of time, and it's helpful to organize these in one place so that they are easily accessible. You can set up separate file folders for each one or group them by category. Some files to keep for a lifetime or until they're no longer needed include:

- ❑ Birth, marriage, and death certificates, divorce papers, wills, trusts, social security cards, and military discharge papers should be kept for life, and you should also

Continued on the next page

keep a backup such as a copy (off-site) with a friend/relative, attorney, in a safe-deposit box, or with an online service like Mozy.com or Carbonite.com

- ❑ Tax returns, while you can shred the documentation after seven years, it's a good idea to keep the actual return indefinitely in case you or your heirs need to refer to them.
- ❑ W-2 forms should be kept until you start drawing Social Security in case there is a discrepancy in your income history.
- ❑ Tax forms relating to retirement accounts should be kept as long as you have funds in those accounts, including Form 8606, which helps you calculate your tax basis for future retirement-plan withdrawals; Form 5498, which shows individual retirement account and Roth IRA contributions; and Form 1099-R, which shows IRA withdrawals.
- ❑ Receipts and documents related to assets such as confirmations showing the purchase price of a stock, titles, or improvements on a house, for example, should be kept for as long as you own the asset, plus seven years.
- ❑ For all loans, including mortgages, keep the year-end summaries until the loans are paid off. Then keep indefinitely the final notice showing a loan has been paid off.
- ❑ Keep insurance policies as long as you have the insurance. And for insurance purposes and warranties, keep receipts and appraisals for big purchases as long as you own the items.
- ❑ Keep year-end retirement-plan statements until you retire and move your funds, and traditional pension information indefinitely.

Continued on the next page

Stuff to Keep Temporarily

- ❑ ATM and bank deposit receipts. Keep them until you reconcile them with your bank statements.
- ❑ Credit card receipts. Once a purchase shows up on your credit card statement, you can shred the slip unless you need it for tax purposes, in which case you can scan it and keep it with that year's tax records.
- ❑ Pay stubs. Shred them once you get your year-end summary.
- ❑ Receipts for minor purchases. Keep them for about three months or until you are sure you will not be returning the item.
- ❑ Utility, phone, and Internet bills. If you aren't writing off a home office, including a portion of your utilities, then you can shred these as soon as you receive next month's bill and see that you received credit for your last payment.
- ❑ Insurance claims. Keep for one year after the claim is paid. However, if you wrote off medical costs or a casualty loss on your taxes, keep the information with that year's tax records.
- ❑ Social Security statements. Keep it until you get a new one. Then shred the old one.

Stuff to Toss Immediately (**Note:** Anything that has your name or personal information on it should be shredded before tossing.)

- ❑ Tax return documentation older than eight years
- ❑ Outdated warranties
- ❑ Insurance polices that are no longer in force
- ❑ Older versions of wills and trusts

RESOURCES & TERMS

- Mozy (www.mozy.com) and Carbonite (www.carbonite.com) —online data backup centers.
- To see the IRS forms mentioned, visit www.irs.gov

Terms

assets: Things you own like investments.

cash management: The efficient management of cash in order to put it to work more quickly and keep the cash in applications that produce income.

debt-to-income ratio: Represents the percent of your income that goes toward paying your debts—the lower the number the better.

gross income: The amount of income you earn before taxes or any other deductions.

liabilities: Things you owe like loans.

net worth: Represents the amount left over when you subtract your liabilities from your assets.

SQUEEZE POINTS:

- ***Squeeze Principle #8: Knowing what you own and what you owe is essential before you add to either list!***
- Knowing where you are at all times financially has its benefits, like simplifying the process of decision making, allowing you to spot potential problems before they become major, and providing you with a basis for evaluating how opportunities that come your way will fit with what you already have.

SQUEEZE POINTS *(continued):*

- Calculating your debt-to-income (DTI) ratio allows you to quickly evaluate the level of income it takes to support your debts. Most lenders recommend an overall ratio of 36 percent or less.
- Your net worth is a snapshot of your financial situation at a point in time. The goal is to increase your net worth, and comparing snapshots taken over time shows you if you're on target.

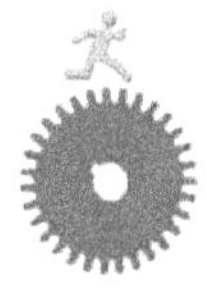

SQUEEZE ACTION ITEMS:

1. Complete the *Squeeze Financial Inventory Worksheet* located in Appendix A and while you have most of your papers out, organize them using the strategies on pp. 147–149. Then using the form on p. 146, calculate your net worth.
2. Calculate your debt-to-income and savings ratios (p. 139 and p. 140).
3. Finally, if you haven't already done so, calculate the amount of money you would have available immediately if an emergency occurred tomorrow (see p. 84) and place a copy in your binder.

Note: the *Squeeze Financial Inventory* is also available online at www.squeezeyourmoney.com

SQUEEZE STORY:

Robert

One of the most difficult things for me to acknowledge is the amount of credit card debt I have, especially since I'm not sure how it happened. It just sneaked up on me. I have been robbing Peter to pay Paul for as long as I can remember, but I had no idea I had so much debt. Between trying to take care of my family and handling some past medical bills, things have just gotten way out of hand. I have been putting off adding it up for years, but I finally did. Once I picked myself up off the floor, I tried to determine where it all came from and then I thought it might be some kind of a huge mistake. As I looked at the mound of debt, I realized that not all of it was necessary. Some of it was to try to make up for the fact that I couldn't give my family everything that they wanted and in some cases things they needed so I started using credit cards, and now it's a habit I'm not sure I can break. Every time I go to buy something, I automatically pull out a card without even considering if I have the money to pay for it in my wallet or bank account. I caught myself the other day starting to charge a candy bar. ENOUGH...it's time for this madness to stop.

CHAPTER TWELVE

DEVELOPING A PERSONAL FINANCIAL GAME PLAN

"Would you tell me, please, which way I ought to go from here?"
asked Alice in Lewis Carroll's Alice in Wonderland.

"That depends a good deal on where you want to get to,"
answered the Cheshire Cat

Squeeze Principle #9: The best way to ensure that you get to where you want to go is to develop a plan and follow it. Anything less could lead you down a totally different path!

While most people would never consider building their dream home without a blueprint or going on a road trip without a map, many often ignore this same principle when it comes to creating a financial plan to help them get to where they want to go. And they opt instead to use the DAYGA (design as you go along) method, which often leaves them disappointed when it comes time to do some of the things they really want to do like purchasing a house, sending their kids to college, or retiring because they find that the resources

USING THE DAYGA (DESIGN AS YOU GO ALONG) METHOD CAN LEAD TO DISAPPOINTMENTS WHEN IT COMES TIME TO DO THINGS YOUR REALLY WANT TO DO...LIKE RETIRE

they need are not available for them to accomplish tasks like these in the manner they had originally imagined.

What's a Financial Game Plan?

A financial game plan is like a map or a blueprint. It starts with an analysis of where you are and where you want to go, and it ends with a sequence of action steps to bridge the gap between the two. Having a financial plan allows you to make efficient use of time and resources because it keeps you from wasting time wondering what to do next and it reduces or eliminates bad money decisions by providing you with a step-by-step guide to follow. Keeping your plan updated means that you can see at a glance how much you have progressed towards your goals and how far you are from your destination. This is essential for making good decisions on where to go or what to do next.

Also, effective planning often allows you to anticipate obstacles that may be coming your way so that you can either adjust your plan to avoid them or at least lessen their impact, which is so much better than facing an unexpected crisis head-on.

Steps to Construct a Financial Plan

Creating and following a personal financial plan or blueprint is a good way to create the financial future you want. And it's not nearly as difficult to construct one as you might expect. You can have a financial professional create one for you or you can create one yourself by following the five-step plan outlined in this chapter.

Note: *A financial plan is a guide so it should be as complete and accurate as possible. If you decide to create one on your own and you get stuck, get help. There are advisors who will work with you on an hourly basis so if you don't want to make a long-term commitment, seek out someone who will answer your questions and get you back on track. (See the Resources & Terms below.)*

RESOURCES & TERMS

Resources for financial advisors and financial planning advice

- CFP - Certified Financial Planner Board www.cfp.net (800) 487-1497
- NAPFA - National Association of Personal Financial Advisors www.napfa.org (847) 483-5400
- FPA - Financial Planning Association www.fpanet.org (800) 322-4237
- FINRA - Financial Industry Regulatory Authority - Resource to check credentials and register complaints. www.finra.org (800) 289-9999

OVERVIEW

1) Determine Where Your Are Now
2) Decide Where You Want To Be
3) Develop a Plan to Fill The Gap between Where You Are and Where You Want to Be
4) Plan for Obstacles
5) Implement and Monitor Your Plan

STEP 1: DETERMINE WHERE YOU ARE NOW

This step establishes a baseline or starting point for all of the other steps, so it's important to start with accurate information. The three most important areas to review are your cash management, your investment, and your *risk management* strategies. Luckily, if you have completed the previous exercises in this book, you have already much of the work you completed.

To complete this step, you will need the following:

- A copy of your *Squeeze* Spending Plan Summary and background worksheets (Debits/Checks, Cash, Credit Card Payments, Flexible Spending Money, and Savings/Investments)
- A copy of your *Squeeze Financial Inventory* (located in Appendix A)
- Copies of your insurance policies, tax returns, will, and any other estate planning documents
- A notebook labeled with the current year to keep your plan worksheets and assemble your plan elements

Once you collect everything, complete the following:

Analyze Your Cash Management

There are three areas of cash management that are especially important in developing a plan—the amount of debt you have, the size of your emergency fund, and the amount of money you have available to put toward funding your goals. Collect information on each of these and complete the *Cash Management Questionnaire* on the next page.

The amount of debt you have is important because in some cases, if you have high levels of debt, it may be more important to concentrate on paying down the debt before funding lower priority goals. Paying off your debt will free up additional dollars to invest toward your goals.

The amount of money you have in your emergency fund is important because you could jeopardize any long-term investment plans if you don't have sufficient funds to cover short-term emergencies. And finally, the amount of money you have available to fund your goals will determine which goals you can fund and at what level.

Squeeze: Cash Management Questionnaire

Instructions: Using information from your spending plan and financial inventory, provide answers to the following questions.

1.	Your total monthly income	
2.	The total amount of money in your emergency fund	
3.	Your total loan balance *(excluding your mortgage)*	
4.	Your total monthly loan payments *(excluding your mortgage)*	
5.	Your total credit card balance	
6.	Your total monthly credit card payments	
7.	Your current monthly savings amount	
8.	Based on your income and expenses, what amount could you commit to save each month to fund your goals?	

Note: Additional copies of all of the planning worksheets can be found on the Squeeze website at www.squeezeyourmoney.com.

Analyze Your Investments

In order to develop your plan, you need specific information about all of your current investments. This will provide you with the information to decide whether or not you need to make changes to your current investments to achieve your goals. You should be able to find most of this information in your *Squeeze Financial Inventory*. You may, however, you may need the help of your stockbroker or investment advisor to complete some of the information.

Using the following explanations, complete the *Investment Analysis Worksheet* on p. 161.

1. **Description**. List the name and a brief description of each investment (e.g., IBM/100 shares).
2. **Year acquired**. When did you purchase the investment?
3. **Cost basis**. What was the amount you originally paid for this investment?
4. **Current value**. What is the current market value of this investment, assuming you sell it today?
5. **Annual return/savings**. How much income did you earn on this investment last year (before taxes)? If the investment was held solely for tax credits or deductions, list the tax dollars you saved. You can use one of the online calculators listed in the Resources & Terms section at the end of Step 1 or you can use the *Annual Investment Return Worksheet* on p. 160 to get an approximate return.
6. **Percent of total portfolio**. Divide the current value (#4) by the total value of your portfolio. For example, if the total value of your portfolio is $20,000 and you have an investment worth $6,000, it represents 30 percent. [6,000 ÷ 20,000 = .30]

7. **Asset type.**[1] What category does each asset fit into? This will show you at a glance if most of your investments fall into one category or if you have a lot of variety or diversity. Well diversified portfolios often lead to better returns. Read more about diversification in Chapter 13. (**Note**: List the asset type by letter.)
    A. **Business interest**. Do you own a business or have an equity interest in another company?
    B. **Fixed income**. This includes money market accounts and funds, CDs, T-bills, and bonds.
    C. **Stocks/ Mutual funds**. This includes growth and income stocks or funds.
    D. **Real estate**. This includes limited partnerships, rental property, or undeveloped property.
    E. **Speculative**. This includes aggressive growth stocks, bonds and mutual funds as well as futures, options, gas and oil, gold and precious metals.
    F. **Collectibles**. This includes artwork, coins, stamps, etc.
    G. **Other**.
8. **Asset objective**. What investment objective are these assets currently meeting? **Note**: List the asset objective by number.
    - -1- Insure safety of principal
    - -2- Provide additional source of current income
    - -3- Provide additional current income to meet specific needs (e.g., purchasing a home)
    - -4- Provide additional future income to meet specific needs (e.g., child's education)
    - -5- Provide future income for retirement
    - -6- Hedge against inflation

[1] If you are unsure of the asset type, you can use the Morningstar's Instant X-Ray tool to help you analyze it at www.morningstar.com on the Tools tab.

-7- Provide a source of emergency funds with an emphasis on liquidity

-8- Minimize current tax consequences

-9- Minimize future tax consequences

-10- Increase value of estate for heirs

Squeeze: Annual Investment Return Worksheet

Instructions: Follow the steps below to get an approximate return on your investments.

	Example	
1. Current account value	*$15,335*	$ ________
2. Account value at the end of last year	*$13,001*	$ ________
3. Subtract line 2 from line 1	*$ 2,334*	$ ________
4. Divide the amount on line 3 by line 2 then multiply by 100	*18%*	________%

Note: To get a more accurate calculation, contact your investment advisor or use one of the online calculators such as those at www.timevalue.com and www.dinkytown.com that allow you to add ongoing contributions and fees.

Analyze Your Risk Management

Although the primary objective of personal financial planning is to increase your net worth, it is equally important to protect your net worth as well. So risk management is key, and the two areas of greatest concerned are the potential loss of income and loss of assets.

RISK MANAGEMENT IS KEY TO PROTECTING YOUR NET WORTH.

Loss of Income

There are three basic ways you might lose your current

Investment Analysis Worksheet

Description	Year Acq'd	Cost Basis	Current Value	Annual Return	% of Total	Asset Type	Asset Objective
Example: IBM/100 shares	*3/2010*	*$13,001*	*$15,335*	*18%*	*30%*	*C*	*5*
Total Portfolio Value							

*See pages 158 and 159 for a instructions to complete this worksheet.

source of income including losing your job, suffering a prolonged illness or disability, or a premature death. So it's important to have insurance and/or strategies in place to eliminate or minimize the effects if one of these events occurs. Some strategies include preparing yourself psychologically by staying open to change and understanding your strengths and weaknesses so you can shore up your weaknesses and play to your strengths; preparing yourself professionally either through additional education or by developing a second career, or even a sideline business that could become a full-time occupation if necessary; and preparing yourself financially with an emergency fund that will cover your expenses during most emergencies so you don't have to liquidate investments you have set aside for other goals like retirement.

PREPARE PSYCHOLOGICALLY, PROFESSIONALLY, AND FINANCIALLY FOR THE POTENTIAL OF LOSS OF INCOME.

Insurance is also an important component. While a lot of people have and understand the importance of life insurance, many are inadequately insured when it comes to disability or income continuation policies. And yet, according to statistics, the chances of becoming temporarily or permanently disabled in your lifetime are nearly twice as great as the risk of a premature death. The purpose of disability insurance is to provide a source of income if you are disabled and cannot work. This protection is particularly important if your salary is the main source of income in your household. A good policy will replace up to 60% of your income. The cost depends on your age, health, occupation, and the specific terms and conditions of the policy.

Many employers offer disability insurance as an option. If you have the option, consider selecting both short- and long-term disability, and be sure you understand the basics of the policy, such as what qualifies as a disability and when benefits are paid. On the other hand, if you have to purchase a policy on your own, be aware that these policies are not inexpensive, however like auto insurance that you may rarely need, it may be well worth the cost.

Life Insurance: If anyone depends on your income and you don't have enough savings to cover their needs, life insurance is a good option to help minimize the financial impact if you should suffer a premature death. The big question is what kind of insurance should you buy, and how much do you need? The answer will depend on a number of factors, including who you want to provide for and how you want to provide for them.

Here are six common reasons people buy life insurance, and over time as your answers to these questions change, you should go back and review your policies to make sure they will still work for you:

- ❑ To provide living expenses for a surviving spouse or dependents either for their lifetime or a limited period of time
- ❑ To provide a lump sum cash inheritance for beneficiaries
- ❑ To provide education funds for dependent children
- ❑ To pay off an existing mortgage or other loans or debts
- ❑ To cover funeral/burial expenses
- ❑ To meet requirements of a buy-sell agreement for a closely held business

Once you understand who and/or what you want to cover with life insurance, you can focus on the type of insurance and the amount you need. Do your homework to understand the different options available and then select policies and coverage amounts that are appropriate for you.

There are two basic types of life insurance available: whole life and term.

Whole life, cash value, or permanent insurance is a combination of insurance and a savings component. Whole life premiums can be costly: however, the insurance covers you for life, and the premiums are intended to remain level for the life of the policy. Only purchase a whole life policy if you plan to be in it for the long-term so that you can realize some of the savings benefits. (**Note:** At your death, your beneficiary receives only the policy's death benefit—not the death benefit and the cash value, and any outstanding loans will be subtracted.)

Term insurance, on the other hand, is just insurance. And because it doesn't come with a lot of bells and whistles like permanent insurance, it's cheaper. Term policies cover you for a fixed period of time—one, five, ten, fifteen, or twenty years. The policies are typically renewable until you're eighty years old. Term premiums start very low and gradually increase as you get older. But you're not locked in; you can drop your policy at any time without incurring a surrender charge.

Some other important areas to consider include the status of your estate planning and tax documents. They should be current, including the beneficiaries, and contain strategies that allow you to pay the least amount of taxes.

Buy Life Insurance to Protect Your Family—Not as an Investment...

Never forget the real purpose of life insurance. Whole life policies are sometimes marketed as a tax-deferred investment. However, if saving or investing is one of your goals, life insurance should be your last option because once you factor in the high ongoing cost of the policy, it will take years to earn as much as you can in some other type of vehicle such as a mutual fund. Always keep your ultimate purpose in mind when purchasing insurance.

Loss of Assets

Since personal assets often represent a large percentage of your net worth, it's important to have adequate coverage for large items like your home and car. While price is certainly a consideration in buying insurance, it shouldn't be your most important consideration. First focus on what the policy does and doesn't cover so you can avoid surprises if you have to file a claim. Think of as many scenarios as possible and ask a lot of questions before you purchase a policy.

BEFORE BUYING INSURANCE FOCUS AS MUCH ON WHAT IT DOESN'T COVER AS WHAT IT DOES TO AVOID SURPRISES IF YOU HAVE TO FILE A CLAIM.

Once you know what a policy does and does not cover then you can make cost comparisons based on the ones that offer more of the features you want. Comparison shopping is essential because costs can vary widely from company to company.

Conduct a Risk-Management Assessment

- ❑ Write out the steps you will follow if you lose your job or if you have to take a pay cut. Consider psychological, professional, and financial strategies. Do this even if the possibility of this occurring seems slim.
- ❑ Establish your risk-management objectives, especially in the area of life insurance.
- ❑ Gather all of your current policies and review them based on your objectives. Review the amount of coverage you need and what the policies actually cover.
- ❑ Identify areas of concern or gaps in coverage.
- ❑ Get new quotes from a variety of companies on policies that are two years or older.
- ❑ Review your estate-planning documents. These should include at a minimum a will that names a guardian if you have minor children, a durable power of attorney, a living will, and a healthcare directive. Also, review the beneficiaries on documents such as your will, life insurance policies and any investment accounts to be sure they are current.
- ❑ Review your last tax return and look for ways to lower your tax bill. If you need help, ask your tax preparer or a financial professional for suggestions.

RESOURCES & TERMS

Online calculators for calculating investment returns

- www.dinkytown.com - www.timevalue.com

Resources for insurance quotes and information:

- Insure.com www.insure.com
- Insurance.com www.insurance.com
- Bankrate.com www.bankrate.com
- Insurance Information Institute www.iii.org
- National Association of Insurance Commissioners www.naic.org

STEP 2: DECIDE WHERE YOU WANT TO BE

This is the fun part of planning because you get to think about and envision what you want your future to look like, so don't skimp on this one. You can opt for traditional goals like buying a house or planning for retirement, you can take a totally different path, or you can mix the traditional with the non-traditional. It's totally up to you! Perhaps you want to retire early and travel every year, or you never want to retire, but you want to move to an exotic place in ten years. Or perhaps you can't see past your debt, and getting out of debt, is your biggest goal. Choose the goals and the future that have the most meaning for you because the more important they are to you, the more motivated you will be to make them a reality.

Next, using the *Goal Priorities Worksheet* on the next page, start a list of the goals you want to accomplish. Use the areas listed as a guide, but don't limit yourself. Write down everything that comes to mind.

Squeeze: Goal Priorities Worksheet

Instructions: Using the areas below as a guide, create a list of goals you would like to accomplish.

1. Personal Goals
   - Assets/possessions ____________________
   - Career changes/ achievements/ business ownership ____________________
   - Lifestyle ____________________
   - Education ____________________
   - Your definition of financial independence ____________________

2. Financial Goals
   - Increase net worth ____________________
   - Investments/increase assets ____________________
   - Major purchases ____________________
   - Savings program ____________________
   - Emergency funds ____________________
   - Reduction of debt ____________________
   - Reduction of taxes ____________________
   - Standard of living ____________________

3. Retirement Plans
   - Age to retire ____________________
   - Retirement funding ____________________
   - Standard of living ____________________
   - Location/type of residence ____________________
   - Lifestyle ____________________
   - Full or partial retirement ____________________
   - Sources of retirement income ____________________

Squeeze: Goal Priorities Worksheet *(continued)*

4. Basics for the Family
   - Standard of living ______________
   - Insurance ______________
   - Education ______________
   - Travel/vacation home ______________
   - Estate assets ______________

   ____

5. Estate Plans
   - Your will ______________
   - Trusts ______________
   - Beneficiaries ______________
   - Assets ______________
   - Tax considerations ______________
   - Charitable contributions ______________
6. Other

   ______________ ______________

   ______________ ______________

After you compile your big list, select the goals you want to work on now and transfer them to the *Goal Planning Worksheet* on p. 171. Include a priority rating of how important they are to you (with #1 as the highest), the total amount needed, a time frame in months (so three years would be thirty-six months), the amount you currently have saved, if any, the monthly amount to save to achieve this goal by the deadline date, and how achieving this goal will impact you and/or your family.

For example, if you have a goal to purchase a house that

costs $200,000 (unless you intend to pay for it in cash), calculate the amount you will need for things like the down payment, closing costs, moving costs, and possibly new furniture or appliances. Then divide that amount by the number of months to get a monthly amount. Don't worry about how you will accomplish it, just write them down, and you can edit yourself later, if necessary.

If you're unsure about the amount of money you will need to accomplish your goal, you may need to do some research. For example, using the example above, purchasing a home, start by researching house prices in the areas that interest you, typical down payments, and closing costs. Real estate agents can be a great resource for this type of information, and there are lots of online resources like www.realtor.com and www.bankrate.com.

Or if a comfortable retirement is one of your goals, begin by defining what a comfortable retirement means in terms of an annual income based on how you plan to spend your days. Then once you have an idea of how much you will need, you can use one of the online calculators like www.dinkytown.com or www.bankrate.com to calculate the total amount you will need along with a suggested monthly savings amount. Some other general research resources include libraries, professionals who work in the area of your goal, community agencies, and the Internet.

STEP 3: DEVELOP A PLAN TO FILL IN THE GAP BETWEEN WHERE YOU ARE NOW AND WHERE YOU WANT TO BE

Now that you have all of the basic information about

GOAL PLANNING WORKSHEET

Priority #	Goal	Total Amount Needed	Number of Months	Current Amount Saved	Monthly Funds Required	Impact of Achieving this Goal
1	*Example: Build an emergency fund*	*$5,000*	*24*	*$3,000*	*$83*	*I won't have to rely on credit cards all the time*

where you are and where you want to go, it's time to develop a plan to fill in the gaps to achieve your goals. Answering questions like the following will help you create an action plan to follow:

- **Which goals will you move forward on?** Review all of the goals you listed on your *Goal Planning Worksheet* and determine the ones you want to start to work on immediately. A good place to start is with the goals you gave a #1 priority. However, even after you make your decisions, keep your *Goal Planning Worksheet* because your needs and wants may change.

  Once you decide on a goal, fill in any missing details. Be sure you have a description that is specific, the total amount of money you will need, a realistic time frame, and an understanding of any other things you will need to do to accomplish it.

- **How will you allocate the funds you have available?** Review the total amount of funds you have available for Savings/Investments in your spending plan and decide if you will allocate it all to one goal or to several goals, and if so, how much you want to allocate to each one.

- **Which investments will you use to fund each goal?** If you are already saving for a goal and you have an investment set aside for the goal, evaluate whether it is the best investment vehicle for the goal. *(If you have questions about which investments work best for different types of goals, see Chapter 13 for more on investments.)* However, for those goals that you do not currently have a savings or investment vehicle, review your options and make a decision so you can get started.

- **What are the steps you need to follow to make your goals a reality?** Review all aspects of the goal, and develop a series of action steps. Remember, there is often more to achieving a goal than just getting the money together, so consider all of the steps you need to follow before, during, and after you accumulate the money.

After you decide on the goals you want to work on, develop a micro or mini plan for each one that incorporates the answers to the questions above along with a timeline. Here is an example of a micro plan:

Bob and Susan: House Goal Micro Plan
Goal: Purchase a $200,000 in 3-years with a 10% down payment.

☑ **Total Amount Needed:** $20,000 down payment
6,000 closing costs
2,000 moving costs
2,000 new appliances
$30,000

☑ **Monthly Amount to Invest:** $300/mo
☑ **Investment Plan:** Current high-yield savings account with a balance of $18,000

Action Steps
☑ Y1: Reseach the neighborhoods of interest
☑ Y1: Place pictures of our dream house everywhere so we know why we are saving
☐ Y2: Decide on a realtor and tell them what we want
☐ Y2: Take homebuyer's class and get pre-qualified
☐ Y2: Attend open houses and begin looking online
☐ Y3: Decide on a house and make an offer

Note: Each year Bob and Susan can review their plans and set exact dates to complete the upcoming steps.

STEP 4: PLAN FOR OBSTACLES

Obstacles are simply a part of achieving most goals. We know they're coming so it only makes sense to plan for them, especially the ones we can anticipate. For example, if you're going on a diet, you already know which foods tempt you the most so you should develop a plan to avoid being around them as much as possible, at least until you can control yourself around them. So if you really like sweets, you probably should avoid bakeries and hanging out in the cookie aisle at the grocery store. And the same is true for achieving financial goals. It's tough enough to save for a future goal so don't tempt yourself by hanging out at the mall (online or offline) with cash or credit cards in hand.

One of the best ways to overcome obstacles is to have a plan to follow. Working on goals you really want and having steps to follow can help you stay on track and avoid many obstacles so as you develop your plan, anticipate as many obstacles as possible and build in strategies to help you sidestep or avoid them altogether. For example, consider carrying only cash (your fun money and no credit cards) when you go shopping with your friends so you can still hangout and have some fun, but not overspend.

However, there are times when staying focused on your goal and following the steps in your plan are not enough. This usually occurs when you lack experience with the goal you want to accomplish, and this can result in a plan that doesn't account for all of the nuisances associated with achieving your goal. Instead of scrapping your plan or allowing an obstacle to derail you, consider flexible planning.

With flexible planning, your plan isn't fixed or static. Instead it evolves, shifts, and changes as you gain experience and learn from your mistakes. Start with your initial plan, and whenever an experience or a mistake throws you off course, change your plan immediately to stay on course. Your plan should always reflect your best ideas or perceptions about what it will take to get from where you are to your end goal. This will help your plan stay relevant so you can still use it as a guide to help you make future decisions.

HOWEVER, THERE ARE TIMES WHEN FOLLOWING THE STEPS IN YOUR PLAN IS NOT ENOUGH SO TO STAY ON TRACK BUILD SOME FLEXIBILITY INTO YOUR PLAN AND MAKE CHANGES AS NEEDED.

STEP 5: IMPLEMENT AND MONITOR YOUR PLAN

Even the best financial plan is just a stack of papers if you don't implement it. So once you have your goals and your micro or mini plans in place, it's time to implement your plan—to follow the action steps you outlined in each micro plan and then to monitor your progress as you accomplish each step. Review your plans at least weekly, and check off tasks you have completed. If your plan requires you to set up savings programs or investments, get started right away because every day you delay means you have less time for your investments to grow. Or if you will be changing insurance policies, be sure to put any new insurance policies in place before you cancel your current one. Also, keep copies of all important correspondence and receipts until you are sure they are no longer needed.

Finally, as challenges or opportunities arise, remember to use your plan as a sounding board so you can determine if acting on them will help or hurt your chances of achieving your goals. Also, plan to review and update your plan at least annually so you can stay on track and on target.

Hey, wait a minute. I'm not quite sure I understand what to do. Can you show me another example of a mini or micro plan?

No problem. This will take some getting used to. Basically, you take each goal and create a separate plan for it. You can then put them together in your notebook, but since they all have different deadlines, steps, and priorities, it will be easier to actually manage them separately. (See the Case Study below.)

CASE STUDY: Emergency Fund Goal

George has a goal to accumulate $5,000 in an emergency fund so that he can stop relying on his credit cards every time something out of the ordinary occurs. However, he is not sure how to set up an investment plan, and he hasn't gotten started because he isn't sure where to start.

Continued on the next page

CASE STUDY: Emergency Fund Goal *(continued)*

Here is George's Micro Plan:

Goal: Accumulate $5,000 in an emergency fund.

☑ **Total Amount Needed:** $5,000

☑ **Monthly Amount to Invest:** $150/mo

☐ **Investment Plan:**

____

Action Steps

☐ Y1: Reseach investment options

☐ Y1: Link checking and savings/investment account so that additions are made automatically each month

Fill in the blank with your best guess. Then see George's solution on page 213.

SQUEEZE POINTS:

- ***Squeeze Principle #9: The best way to ensure that you get to where you want to go is to develop a plan and follow it. Anything less could lead you down a totally different path!***
- A financial plan is like a roadmap or a blueprint that starts with where you are and charts a course to where you want to be.
- The five basic steps involved in creating a financial game plan include:
  - Determine Where Your Are Now
  - Decide Where You Want To Be

Continued on the next page

SQUEEZE POINTS *(continued):*

- Develop a Plan to Fill the Gaps between Where You Are and Where You Want To Be
- Plan for Obstacles
- Implement and Monitor Your Plan

▶ Once you collect all of the basic information, you can begin to build micro or mini plans for each of your major goals. Micro plans include all of the details about your goals, including the action steps to complete them.

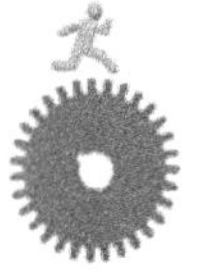

SQUEEZE ACTION ITEMS:

1. Build a personal financial plan to follow. Start by collecting information about your current situation and completing the following worksheets and a micro or mini plan for each goal. (See p. 173 for a micro plan example.)

2. Complete the following worksheets

- ❑ Cash Management Questionnaire
- ❑ Investment Analysis Worksheet
- ❑ Goal Planning Worksheet

3. Fill in the blank on George's Micro Plan *(See p. 176.)* Then see George's solution on p. 213.

Note: Blank copies of the worksheets are available at www.squeezeyourmoney.com

CHAPTER THIRTEEN

CRAFTING AN INVESTMENT PROGRAM THAT FITS YOU

"October. This is one of the particularly dangerous months to speculate. The others are July, January, September, April, November, May, March, June, December, August, and February."

— Mark Twain

"So don't speculate, do your homework and pick investments you can stand behind."

— Patricia Stallworth

Squeeze Principle #10: Investing is not just for the wealthy— it's also for those who want to get that way so get started sooner rather than later!

Investing is one of the quickest and easiest ways to build wealth and a secure financial future. If you haven't yet taken the plunge, there's no time like the present. But first take the time to educate yourself about investments even if you intend to have someone else manage them for you. In today's world, you just can't afford to not know everything about your investments—from the basics like exactly what you're invested in and how much it cost—to specifics like why a particular investment is a good fit for you and the level of risk it has—to how this investment reacts in different markets and how it will interact with other investments you own. Always stay involved and ask questions if you don't understand. Anything less is just too risky.

7 Investment Basics

Getting started with an investment program is one of the best ways to grow your money. However, before you start a program, here are seven basics to consider and/or put in place so that once you get started, you can hit the ground running and not look back.

ALL INVESTMENTS HAVE RISK, EVEN THE SO-CALLED 'SAFE' ONES.

First, all investments have risk, even the so-called "safe" ones. However, not all investments are created equal when it comes to risk, so it's important to understand the level of risk of each investment before you purchase it. Whether you buy small pieces of companies (stocks or equities) or lend money to companies and/or governments (bonds or debt instruments), your money is only as secure as the company or companies you invest in.

In addition to the soundness of the company, investments also depend on general economic conditions, both in the U.S. and around the world. And if you're not prepared to take the risk that your investments could be worth less tomorrow or next year than they are today, then perhaps you should only invest in very "safe" investments like bank savings accounts, CDs, money market accounts, and US Treasury bonds. However, the tradeoff (or the risk) with these investments is that your money will grow very slowly, and when you factor in inflation and taxes, you could end up with less purchasing power, which can have the same impact as losing money. So don't ignore your risk-tolerance level but also take into account the risk that you might not achieve your goals if you only select very "safe" investments. Instead try reach a compromise by taking on more risk with at least a portion of your portfolio so you can enjoy as many of the benefits of investing as possible.

What's the Real Difference Between a 4 Percent and a 5 Percent Return?

When asked this question, most people believe the answer is 1%. While that is a correct answer, the difference, stated more accurately, is one percentage point, making the real difference 25 percent. [5 ÷ 4 = 1.25 or a 25 percent increase]

To see how this works, let's assume you had an investment earning 4 percent and you were receiving a monthly check of $400 from this money. If you moved the money to an investment earning 5 percent, would your monthly check just increase by 1 percent to $404? No, your check would increase by ¼ or 25 percent to $500 [400 × .25 = 100]. So you see, just a few percentage points difference in your return can make a substantial difference in the growth of your money. See the chart below for more examples.

Growth Chart for Investing $1,200 Annually ($100 per month)

# of Years	Amount Invested	Rate of Return			
		5%	7%	9%	11%
5	$6,000	$6,809	$7,160	$7,527	$7,912
10	$12,000	$15,499	$17,202	$19,109	$21,243
20	$24,000	$40,746	$51,041	$64,346	$81,561

Second, the real purpose of investing is to fund your goals. Investing without goals is like going on a trip with no real destination in mind—you may never get there. So set goals with specific dollar amounts. Your goals are one of the three main factors that will help you determine the best types of investments to reach your goals.

THE REAL PURPOSE OF INVESTING IS TO FUND YOUR GOALS. INVESTING WITHOUT GOALS IS LIKE BUILDING A HOUSE WITHOUT A BLUEPRINT.

Another factor that will help you determine which investments are best to achieve your goals is what you want your money to do or the objective. The three main objectives that most people want are for their money to grow, to remain stable because they will need it soon, or to provide them with an income stream. For example, in retirement, you may want an income stream to supplement your income. And, if you're saving to buy a car next year, while you might like for your money to grow, your main objective is for the money to be there when you need it, so preservation of capital is your main objective.

Third, your time frame or when you will need the money should be considered before you choose investments. Some goals are short-term (three years or less), while others are mid-term (three to seven years), and still others may be long-term (seven-plus years). In general, the shorter your time frame, the more important it is to choose investments that will preserve your principal such as CDs and money market funds; otherwise, you run the risk that the market will be down when you need the money and you could miss your goal. However, if you won't need the money from your investment(s) for a longer period of time, you have the flexibility to choose from a variety of investments. So look for investments that have enough potential for growth to outpace inflation and taxes to maintain your purchasing power. And, if growth is your main objective, consider investments that have the potential to grow beyond just maintaining your purchasing power. Ultimately, your time frame can help you decide how much risk you can afford to take to reach your goals, and it is the third factor to consider in choosing the best investments to achieve your goals.

Fourth, it's important to have or at least start an emergency fund before you get started with a long-term investment program. An emergency fund is basically a stash of cash that you have set aside to cover unexpected expenses that come up like car repairs or a short-term illness that prevents you from working. Having an emergency fund in place lessens the chances that you will have to liquidate your long-term investments to cover unexpected expenses that come up as a part of everyday life. At least a portion of your emergency fund should be available in highly *liquid* investments like savings accounts, CDs, and money market accounts so that the funds will be there when you need them. (See p. 83 for more information on setting up an emergency fund goal.)

Fifth, use *asset allocation* to simplify the process of building a portfolio. Asset allocation provides a plan or model you use in selecting investments. It tells you what percentage of your portfolio to put in stocks, how much in bonds, and how much in cash. As an added benefit, following the plan allows you to get the maximum return for the amount of risk you are taking. Asset allocation is thought by many to be the biggest determiner of your overall portfolio return so it's a big deal.

Hey, wait a minute. I'm confused what does an asset allocation look like and how do I know what a good one is?

Good question, Harvey. In general, a good asset allocation model should consider your goals, your time frame, your risk-tolerance level, or a combination of these. And the recommended percentages of cash, stocks, and bonds should fall into the following ranges: (See the sample models below based on risk tolerance levels below.)

- Cash: 10% to 25%
- Stocks: 40% to 80%
- Bonds: 20% to 50%

Note the change in the percent of stocks as the portfolios progress from conservative to aggressive. Stocks offer the greatest potential for growth, so while increasing the percent of stocks increases your risk, it also increases your potential for growth. In most cases, there is a direct correlation between risk and reward. *(See also the Risk vs. Reward chart on p. 186.)*

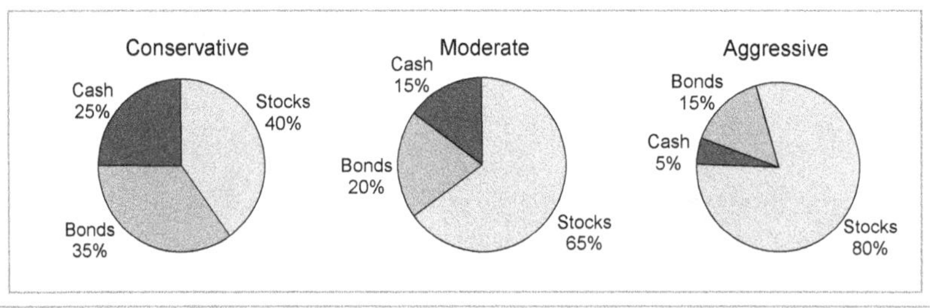

While everyone agrees that asset allocation is important, very few agree on the best one or the best method to use, and if you think about it, it's not difficult to understand why—every size definitely doesn't fit all. There are three basic types of asset allocation models: those that provide a basic model for you to follow; those based on the amount of risk you can tolerate; and those based on the return you will need to meet your goal. There is no one right choice, so choose the method that fits your needs or review them all and then make a decision. Asset allocation is a much of an art as it is a science, so choose the one that fits you best. *(See the Resources & Terms section for asset allocation model links.)*

Sixth, once you establish an asset allocation plan and fund it with investments, check it annually to see if it needs *rebalancing*. Rebalancing allows you to bring investment categories that have strayed from your original target allocations back in line. To stick with your allocation and maintain the percentages, you will need to buy more of the investments that have fallen in value and sell those that have gained. And when you do, you will be buying investments when they are cheaper and selling them at a higher price (remember, buy low/sell high). For example, if your plan calls for a 50/50 split between stocks and bonds and you ended the year with a 55/45 split, simply sell enough stocks and buy bonds to return your portfolio to 50/50. If you have individual stocks and bonds or mutual funds from different companies, you will need to physically sell them; however, if they are all in the same family of funds from one mutual fund company, this may only involve a simple exchange.

Risk vs. Reward

All investments have risk, but some have more than others. Although there are some exceptions, the level of risk and *potential* reward tend to move together so as you move up the pyramid below the level of risk becomes greater and so does the potential reward.

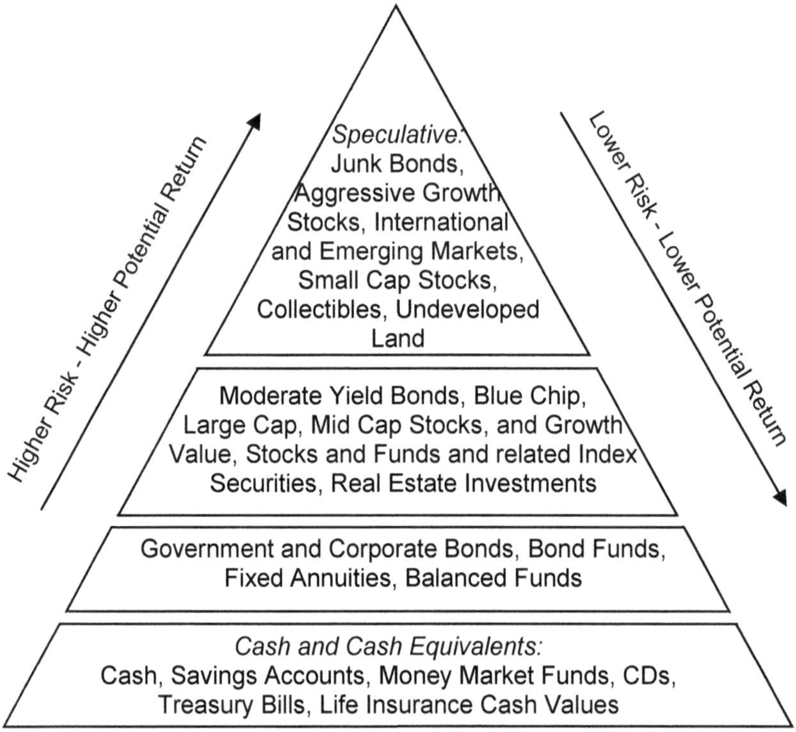

Note: The types of investments listed in each section are only guidelines. The actual level of risk of any specific investment will vary based on a number of factors so always be sure you understand the risks before you invest.

Seventh, investing requires a level of discipline both in sticking with your plan once you get started and in continuing to be vigilant in monitoring your investments and their progress. This includes things like checking statements to be sure that your contributions and purchases have been reported accurately and actually comparing the returns to your projections to see if you are on track, ahead, or falling behind. Don't worry if all of this seems a little overwhelming. It will all come clearer with practice and asking specific questions when you don't understand. So part of the discipline includes continuing to educate yourself.

Hey, wait a minute. What's the difference between asset allocation and diversification?

Good question, Harvey. Asset allocation is the first step in deciding the right mix of basic securities or asset categories for your investment—one that balances risk and reward against your goals. For example, let's say you decide to allocate 60 percent of your retirement savings to stocks and 40 percent to bonds.

The next step is to decide on the specific investments within each category. This process is called diversification. In the example above, if you decided to allocate 60 percent of your retirement savings to stocks. You diversify by selecting several different types of stocks like large cap, small cap, and international. The more diversified your portfolio is, the less likely any one investment choice can hurt you if it performs poorly. And the key is to identify investments in segments of each asset category that may perform differently under the same market conditions.

RESOURCES & TERMS

Asset Allocation Models:

Basic Model: These are general purpose asset allocation models that will work for most people. Some online resources include:

- Financial Calculators from KJE Computer Solutions at www.dinkytown.com in the investment calculators section.

- Smart Money at www.smartmoney.com/investing/basics/investors-allocate-assets-balance-portfolios-at-smartmoneycom-12958

Risk-Based Model: These models suggest asset mixes based on your risk tolerance. Some online resources include:

- Vanguard's Investor Questionnaire at https://personal.vanguard.com/us/FundsInvQuestionnaire

- Index Fund Advisors at www.ifa.com/surveynet/?src=homeicon

Goals-Based Model: These models suggest asset mixes based on your goals and time frame. Some online resources include:

- MSN Money's Asset Allocator at www.moneycentral.msn.com/investor/calcs/assetall/main.asp

- TIAA CREF's Asset Allocation Evaluator at https://ais2.tiaa-cref.org/cgi-bin/WebObjects.exe/DTAssetAlcEval

Terms

asset allocation: The process of allocating your portfolio into the different types of securities: cash, stocks or equities, and bonds or fixed income.

cash equivalents: These include any type of investment that can easily be converted into cash with little or no loss of principal like CDs, money market accounts and funds, Treasury bills, and commercial paper.

diversification: Allocation of the investments in your portfolio within the categories of stocks, bonds, and cash.

Continued on the next page

RESOURCES & TERMS (continued)

- *liquid investment:* an investment that can be converted to cash quickly with little or no loss of principal.
- *rebalancing*: to buy and sell securities so as to maintain a predetermined ratio of selected categories in an investment account based on your asset allocation.

Investing in Stocks, Bonds, Mutual Funds, and ETFs

In all probability whenever someone mentions investing, one of the first things that pops into your head is investing in stocks and the ups and downs of the stock market. But investing is not just about picking stocks—it's so much more. In fact, you don't even have to invest in individual stocks to build a diversified portfolio to achieve your goals.

We will review the basics of investing in stocks, bonds, mutual funds, and ETFs so you can start to build an investment program or evaluate the investments you already own. Then you can check out other resources to dig more deeply into the areas that interest you most.

STOCKS

When you buy a share of stock in a company, you're actually buying a part ownership in it, and you get to share in a portion of the company's assets and its profits. While one share of stock doesn't usually represent a very large portion of ownership, especially in a large corporation which could have hundreds of millions of shares outstanding, you still own a share of the company.

Generally you can make money in stock in one of two ways—through *appreciation,* or the increase of a stock's price over time, or *dividends,* a portion of a company's profit paid out to eligible shareholders on a per-share basis.

There are several different types of stocks:

- *Large-cap* – Stocks issued by large companies with a *market capitalization* (outstanding shares times the stock price) over $10 billion.
- *Mid-cap* – Stocks issued by midsized companies with a *market capitalization* less than $10 billion.
- *Small-cap* – Stocks issued by smaller companies with a *market capitalization* of less than $1 billion.
- *International* – Stocks issued by companies in other countries, including emerging markets (like China, India, and Mexico) and developed markets (like the United Kingdom, Germany, and France).
- *Growth* – Stocks whose value may grow higher than other stocks, or even the market as a whole.
- *Value* – Stocks that cost less than you might expect based on things like dividends, earnings, sales, etc. In other words, they are considered bargains or undervalued.
- *REITs* – These are dividend paying stocks that focus on real estate.

You can buy and sell stocks through a full-service, discount, or online broker who conducts the transaction on your behalf through either a *listed exchange* like the New Your Stock Exchange (NYSE) or one of the *over-the-counter markets* like Nasdaq.

One of the best strategies to get started investing in stocks is to invest in things you know or things that interest you. Consider the places you shop (like T.J. Maxx), places you play (like Disneyland), or your hobbies, etc. If you like a product or service, chances others do also. Consider what you like about it, and then do your homework. This is why it should be something you like or are interested in because you need to find out as much about the company as possible before you invest. Your homework, at a minimum, should include reading any company plans, news, and annual reports. Your goal should be to select stocks that you feel will be around for a long time so you can invest in them for the long-term (ten to twenty years or more).

While it's great to invest in individual stocks, it's not always practical, especially for new investors or those with limited funds. One option is to invest in stock mutual funds (a collection of individual stocks sometimes as many as one-hundred or more). This gives you some of the same benefits of investing in individual stocks (the potential for growth) with less risk because if one stock goes down, it will have less of an impact on your total investment.

RESOURCES & TERMS

Stock Terms:

bear market: A prolonged decline in the overall market value of stocks, usually 20 percent or more.

blue chip: A particularly high-quality stock, usually issued by a large company with a long history of stable earnings and profitability. Examples include companies like Coca-Cola and General Electric.

bull market: A prolonged increase in the overall market value of stocks, usually 20 percent or more.

common stock: The most basic form of stock. Common stock usually gives shareholders the right to vote on important matters to the corporation, such as membership on the board of directors, with one vote for each individual share of stock owned.

dividend: A payment that a corporation makes to its shareholders out of its profits for a given period of time.

Dow Jones Industrial Average (DJIA): The most commonly used indicator of overall US stock market health and vitality. The average is based a price-weighted average of 30 blue-chip stocks chosen by the editors of *the Wall Street Journal.*

initial public offering (IPO): The initial offering of a company's stock to the public, such as when Google offered its stock for sale to the public for the first time on August 19, 2004, raising more than $1.5 billion for the company.

market capitalization: The value of a company on the stock market. This figure is determined by multiplying the total number of shares of company stock issued by the share price. For example, a company with 1 million shares outstanding, with a share price of $10, has a total market capitalization of $10 million.

penny stock: Generally a stock that sells for less than $1 a share. Many investors buy penny stocks hoping that their value will increase dramatically one day.

Continued on the next page

RESOURCES & TERMS (continued)

preferred stock: Stock that gives its owners priority in the payment of dividends or in the event of liquidation (sale and dismantling) of the company.

price-to-earnings (P/E) ratio: The current market price of a share of stock divided by its earnings (profit) per share over the previous 12 months. Investors can often use this ratio to determine and compare the relative value of different company stocks.

share price: The price to buy one share of stock. The share price for any given stock fluctuates from day to day or even minute to minute based on general economic conditions and expectations, as well as industry or company news or events.

split: When a company increases the number of shares of stock outstanding without changing the proportionate of individual shareholders. For example, in a two-for-one split, 100 shares of stock with a current price of $10 per share and a total value of $1,000 become 200 shares at a price per share of $5 and still worth $1,000. A reverse split works in the opposite direction, by decreasing the number of shares of stock and increasing the price per share.

yield: The annual rate of return of a stock, generally expressed as a percentage.

Note: More terms can be found online at www.investopia.com

BONDS

A bond is basically a loan to a corporation or government agency. You generally receive interest payments until the bond matures and then you receive the principal amount or face value of the bond. Unlike stocks that can vary widely in their returns, bonds are generally stable with more predictable returns that can provide a constant income stream.

There are several different types of bonds:

- *Corporate bonds* are issued by companies to raise capital. Corporate bonds generally have higher rates of return than government bonds because they carry more risk.
- *Municipal bonds* or "munis" — Bonds issued by state, local, or city governments for capital improvement projects. Interest paid to bondholders is often exempt from federal, state, and local income taxes, so even though the return is generally less than corporate bonds, their tax-exempt status can add to your total return.
- *Treasury bonds and notes* — Longer-term bonds issued by the federal government with maturities of 10 years or more. These bonds are backed by the full faith and credit of the US government and are considered to be one of the safest investments available. Interest earned on Treasury bonds is free of state and local taxes.
- *Zero coupon bonds* — Bonds that do not interest. They are attractive because they are generally sold at a significant discount from their par value so that when the bond matures you can make a significant return on their investment.
- *Junk bonds* – Bonds issued by companies with low credit ratings (BBB, Baa, or below). They tend to have more risk and promise higher potential returns. *(See more about bond ratings on the next page.)*

Like stocks, not all bonds are created equal when it comes to risk. Bonds are rated on their quality or level of risk by a variety of independent third-party organizations like Standard and Poor's (www.standardandpoors.com) and Moody's (www.moodys.com). In general, bonds are rated from AAA/Aaa (the best) to D (the worst, which means they are in default). Bonds with ratings below BBB/Baa are considered speculative or junk bonds.

Bonds are generally sold in two different markets—the primary and the secondary market. The primary market is where the government or companies first issue a bond. Buyers (generally brokers) purchase them directly from the issuer and the issuer generally sets the price.

The secondary market is where you can sell bonds before they mature. Prices for bonds can vary significantly from their initial price in the primary market for a variety of reasons, including expectations for future interest rates, economic conditions, and the amount of time remaining before the bond matures. (**Note:** The price of bonds generally varies inversely with interest rates, i.e., as interest rates decrease, the price of bonds goes up because the stated return on the bond becomes more attractive.)

Bonds can be purchased through a broker, or in the case of U.S. Treasury securities, through the Treasury Direct Program of the Federal Reserve.

Like stocks, another option to own bonds is through bond mutual funds. The one thing to keep in mind is that, unlike individual bonds, there is no maturity date with bond mutual funds, so there is no big payoff date.

One of the best ways to compare bonds is to calculate the yield for each one. Here's an example of how to calculate the yield:

The yield on a bond with a par value of $1,000, a current price of $900, and a coupon of rate of 10 percent, is 11 percent. [Yield = $100* ÷ 900 = 0.11 = 11 percent]

*A coupon rate of 10 percent would receive $100 a year in interest payments.

RESOURCES & TERMS

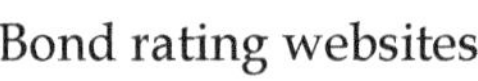

Bond rating websites:
- Standard and Poor's (www.standardandpoors.com)
- Moody's (www.moodys.com).
- Treasury Direct Program to purchase bonds directly from the federal government - www.treasurydirect.gov

Bond Terms:

coupon rate: The interest rate paid to bondholders as a percentage of par value. For example, a bond with a par value of $1,000 with a 10 percent coupon rate pays a bondholder $100 a year until the bond reached maturity. Payments may be made monthly, quarterly, semiannually, or annually, depending on the specific terms.

maturity date: The date on which the issuer promises to return the par value of the bond.

par value: The amount of money that is returned to the bondholder when bond matures. It may also be referred to as the principal or face value.

price: The actual cost of the bond to a buyer in the open market. The price may be above, below, or at par value depending on the market.

yield: The rate of return. The coupon rate divided by the price of the bond.

MUTUAL FUNDS

Mutual funds are collections of stocks, bonds, and cash. One of the reasons for their popularity is that they allow the average investor to participate in the market much like a large investor with a portfolio of investments (which may result in instant diversification), a professional manager who makes buy and sell decisions, and you can get in or out of the market at any time (marketability), all for a fraction of the cost of purchasing the individual investments and hiring an investment manager. Because mutual funds are collections of cash, stocks, and bonds, they are available in every type of security within each of these categories plus a variety of combinations like balanced funds which typically include some of all three. Each mutual fund has an objective aimed at one or a combination of three general areas: growth, income, or safety (preservation of capital). The fund's objective will be stated in the prospectus, and the fund manager will make buy and sell decisions based on the fund's objective. The one real drawback of mutual funds is that some have very high fees, and these fees come out before your profit is calculated, so watch the fees.

> MUTUAL FUNDS ALLOW THE AVERAGE INVESTOR TO PARTICIPATE IN THE MARKET LIKE A LARGE INVESTOR WITH A PORTFOLIO OF INVESTMENTS AND AN INVESTMENT MANAGER.

(Note: To get a better idea of the different types of funds available, review the types of stocks on p. 189 and bonds on p. 193.)

How You Make Money with Mutual Funds

When choosing a mutual fund, one of the most important factors is how it generates a return. You can earn money from your investment in three ways:

(1) **Dividend payments** - If a fund earns income in the form of dividends and interest on the securities it holds, it will distribute the majority of those to shareholders.

(2) **Capital gains distributions** - When the price of the securities a fund owns increases and it sells them, the fund will have a capital gain. At the end of the year, most funds distribute these capital gains (minus any capital losses) to investors.

(**Note**: When you receive dividend payments and capital gains distributions, funds will usually give you the option to either receive a check or other form of payment, or to *reinvest* them in the fund to buy more shares. Regardless of your decision, you may owe taxes on the distributions.)

(3) **You sell your shares for more than you paid for them.**

Five Parts of a Mutual Fund to Review Before You Invest

All mutual funds come with a *prospectus* (a booklet that describes a mutual fund's goals, fees, risks, policies, and investment style). Before you invest, review the prospectus, and, at a minimum, check the following:

1. **The fund's objective**. Not all mutual funds have the same objective. Check to be sure that the one you choose has an objective that matches what you want to accomplish, such as growth, current income, capital preservation, or some combination of these.

2. **The fund manager.** Forget about what's hot and look for a fund with a stable manager that has been around for a while and has a track record of at least five years with the fund. That way you know who is responsible for the track record.
3. **The long-term performance of the fund**. While past performance is no guarantee of future performance, it does provide an indication of how the fund *might* perform in the future. Start with funds that have at least a ten-year track record. Funds with a long track record have experienced both up and down markets, and you can see how they performed in both.
4. **The overall fee and expense structure of the fund**. Fees vary from fund to fund. And the overall goal is to keep them as low as possible because they come out of your profit. Even small differences in fees can translate into large differences in your returns over time. For example, if you invested $10,000 in a fund that produced a 10 percent annual return, but had annual operating expenses of 1.5 percent, after 20 years you would have roughly $49,725. But if that same fund had expenses of only 0.5 percent, then you would end up with $60,858—more than an $11,000 difference. So it's important to select funds with low fees. In fact, always try to look for funds with overall fee structures of 1 percent or less.
5. **The fund's turnover ratio.** The turnover ratio measures how long a fund holds onto the stocks it buys. A high turnover ratio can mean more capital gains and more taxes to pay. Funds that have a turnover ratio of 100 percent are essentially buying a completely new set of companies every year. So look for funds with low turnover

ratios of 50 percent or less when possible.

How to Buy and Sell Mutual Fund Shares

You can purchase shares of some mutual funds by contacting the fund directly. Other mutual fund shares are sold mainly through brokers, banks, financial planners, or insurance agents. All mutual funds will redeem *(buy back)* your shares on any business day and they must send you the payment within seven days.

The easiest way to determine the value of your shares is to call the fund's toll-free number or visit the fund website. The financial pages of major newspapers sometimes print the *NAVs* (prices) for various mutual funds. When you buy shares, you pay the current NAV per share plus any fee the fund assesses at the time of purchase, such as a purchase sales load or other type of purchase fee. When you sell your shares, the fund will pay you the NAV, minus any fee the fund assesses at the time of redemption, such as a deferred (or back-end) sales load or redemption fee. A fund's NAV goes up or down daily as its holdings change in value.

Hey, wait a minute. I heard that index funds were the best way to go because most mutual funds don't beat the market. Is that true?

Yes. Studies have shown that the majority of actively managed mutual funds don't perform as well as the market in most years. And once they subtract the fees from

Continued on the next page

Harvey's Question *(continued)*

your account, it reduces your profit even further. So, yes, there is a great case for using index funds, especially in the areas of large stocks and bonds because there is so much information available that it is hard for fund managers to get an edge, and since there is very little management involved, the fees tend to be really low. Some good examples are the Standard & Poor's 500 Index and the Wilshire 5000 Index (which includes just about every stock on the New York, American, and Nasdaq stock exchanges).

However, remember that because index funds duplicate a market benchmark they will generally do no better than the market, so if the market is down, the index will be down. On the other hand, there are still gems out there that outperform the market. And don't forget about asset allocation. Index funds are a great way to get started, but don't use them exclusively. Once you have $5,000 or $10,000 invested in them, try diversifying into other areas. Do your homework and look for the gems.

RESOURCES & TERMS

- Morningstar - this is a great resource. They have both a paid and a free membership option. Get access to reports and tools to select funds and manage your portfolio.

Mutual Fund Terms:

12B-1 fee: An annual marketing or distribution fee on a mutual fund. The 12b-1 fee is considered an operational expense and is included in a fund's expense ratio. It is generally between 0.25-1% (the maximum allowed) of a fund's net assets.

annual turnover rate: The percentage rate at which a mutual fund or exchange-traded fund replaces its investment holdings on an annual basis.

RESOURCES & TERMS (continued)

automatic reinvestment plan: An investment program in which capital gains or other income received from investments are automatically used for reinvestment purposes. In the case of a mutual fund, for example, capital gains produced by the fund would be used to automatically purchase more shares, instead of being distributed to the investor as cash.

dividend yield: The yield you can expect when you purchase a dividend paying stock. To calculate the dividend yield, divide the annual dividend by the current stock price. For example: If XYZ fund was trading for $10 per share and paid a $1 dividend the dividend yield would be 10% [1 ÷ 10 = .10].

expense ratio: The percentage of total assets used to pay for fund expenses.

load: A fund that comes with a sales charge or commission. The fund investor pays the load, which goes to compensate a sales intermediary (broker, financial planner, investment advisor, etc.) for his or her time and expertise in selecting an appropriate fund for the investor. The load is either paid up front at the time of purchase (front-end load), when the shares are sold (back-end load), or as long as the fund is held by the investor (level-load).

no-load: A fund in which shares are sold without a commission or sales charge. The reason for this is that the shares are distributed directly by the investment company, instead of going through a secondary party.

net asset value (NAV): A mutual fund's price per share or exchange-traded fund's (ETF) per-share value. In both cases, the per-share dollar amount of the fund is calculated by dividing the total value of all the securities in its portfolio, less any liabilities, by the number of fund shares outstanding.

prospectus: Every mutual fund issues a prospectus (a booklet) that describes the investment style of the fund, and answers essential questions like: what kinds of returns has the fund delivered for investors in the past, the fees, and a list of investments or investment types.

RESOURCES & TERMS (continued)

yield: A measure of net income (dividends and interest) earned by the securities in the fund's portfolio less fund expenses during a specified period. A fund's yield is expressed as a percentage of the maximum offering price per share on a specified date.

More terms can be found online at www.investopia.com

Hey, wait a minute. I keep hearing about lifecycle funds. What are they and is that something I should be in?

Good question, Harvey. Lifecycle funds, also know as targeted or age-based funds are growth mutual funds for retirement that are targeted to cycle down to a more conservative level as you get closer to retirement. They are basically a fund of funds. In other words, large companies like Fidelity and Vanguard use combinations of their current funds to create these targeted funds. The idea is that you can select one of these funds at any age and invest in it, and it will mature as you mature. Once you make a decision, there's nothing to do over the years except continue to invest in it—no rebalancing, nothing. How easy is that?

Should you invest in them? Possibly, but proceed with caution. On the one hand, they offer you an easy way to invest for your retirement, and that may the best option if you have no interest in actively investing. However, remember, if something sounds too good to be true, in many cases it is. Here's the problem I have, aside from the expense (these tend to have higher expenses, which ultimately translates into lower profits for you), these funds can be all over the place in terms of the securities they have inside. Some are overly conservative and some are overly aggressive, so you

Continued on the next page

Harvey's Question *(continued)*

need to know the types of securities it owns. Also, it's tough to find one mutual fund company with winners in all categories, so you might not get the best of the best in your target fund. And finally, it's tough to know how to classify or coordinate them with the rest of your portfolio. We've already talked about the how important asset allocation is for your overall portfolio return, and this can be a challenge with lifecycle funds. So if you decide to proceed, look before you leap.

Load vs. No-Load Mutual Funds

Over the years the fees associated with buying mutual funds have gone through a number of changes and there are now so many possibilities. But the two main categories remain, load and no-load. My preference is no-load because there is no evidence that funds with a load perform any better than those without one. But I have two caveats. First, if you are working with someone and they are advising you then the load is a way of paying for their services. And the second one refers to #4 on the p. 199—check the fees. Some no-load funds are now loading up on fees inside the fund, so don't get lulled into thinking that just because you don't have to pay to get in that there are no fees or that it is a cheap fund to be in. Always read the fine print!

ETFs (EXCHANGE-TRADED FUNDS)

An exchange-traded fund (EFT) is simply a basket of securities (stocks or bonds), that's designed to track a segment of the market. It may follow a broad-based index such as the Standard & Poor's 500, or a more specialized area, such as healthcare companies or Chinese stocks.

ETFs are similar to index mutual funds and offer the same advantages of diversification and convenience that make mutual funds such a popular investment choice. However, there are some major differences. For example, ETFs are traded throughout the day just like a stock on the major exchanges, and the price changes throughout the day as the value of the underlying investments change, while the value of mutual fund shares are only calculated at the end of each day, and shares can only be purchased or redeemed only once a day at that price.

Also, ETFs tend to have lower expenses than mutual funds, even index mutual funds, primarily due to the way mutual fund shares are issued. And ETFs have no minimum investment requirements. You can buy a single share. However, they are as risky or conservative as the securities they hold, so before you purchase a specific ETF, ask the same questions as you would with a mutual fund. Get a copy of the prospectus and read it. Determine which index the fund tracks, its largest holdings, and the fees, for example. Also, look at present and past performance and at its total assets. In general, funds with larger assets will charge lower fees. One of the most widely known ETFs is called the Spider (SPDR), which tracks the S&P 500 Index and trades under the symbol SPY. It's been around since 1993 and is a good example to look at if you are new to ETFs.

(Note: See Mutual Funds for common terms)

ETFs vs. Index Mutual Funds

While there are many similarities between ETFs and index mutual funds, there are some occasions when one might be a better fit for you than the other. For example, ETFs tend to be better if you plan to hold an investment for a long time or you have a lump sum of money to invest at one time. This is because of the low fee structures of most ETFs.

On the other hand, index mutual funds tend to work better if you only have only a small amount to invest and/or you like to invest on a regular basis using *dollar-cost averaging. (Read the article below to learn more about dollar cost averaging.)* This is because most ETFs charge you a commission every time you buy and sell shares just like stocks while you can purchase many mutual funds directly from the fund company, avoiding these charges.

Automate Your Investing with Dollar-Cost Averaging!

Automating your investing will make it easy and almost effortless to grow your money, and dollar-cost averaging is a great way to accomplish this. With dollar-cost averaging, you consistently invest each month by having your employer, banker, broker, or mutual fund company deduct a specific amount and invest it in a mutual fund, or other investment. And you have them do this each month regardless of whether the market is up or down. Not only

Continued on the next page

does this technique make investing easy, but you may actually spend less on your investments over time because when the market is down, you will be able to buy more for the same amount of money.

Here is an example of how dollar-cost averaging works:

Sharon authorized her mutual fund company to deduct $100 from her checking account on the 15th of every month to purchase $100 worth of shares of XYZ mutual fund. When the price goes down, more shares are purchased, and when the price goes up, fewer shares are purchased. Here is how Sharon's mutual fund performed over the past six months:

Here is what Sharon's mutual fund account looked like:

Date	Amount Invested	Price per Share	# of Shares Purchased
Jan 15	$100	$10	10.000
Feb 15	$100	$9	11.111
Mar 15	$100	$5	20.000
Apr 15	$100	$6	16.667
May 15	$100	$8	12.500
Jun 15	$100	$10	10.000
Total	$600	48	80.278

Average price per share = $8.00 (48 ÷ 6 months)
Sharon's Average cost per share = $7.47 ($600 ÷ 80.278)
Account balance in June = $802.78 (80.278 x $10 per share)

Sharon was not only able to grow her investments on a regular basis with very little effort, but she also saved money in the process because dollar-cost averaging allowed her to pay less than the overall price per share.

Hey, wait a minute. You haven't mentioned IRAs. What type of investments are they?

Good question, Harvey. IRAs aren't actually a type of investment. They are a type of account that you fund with investments of your choice. IRAs grow tax deferred and that means that they grow faster, so they are a good way to supplement your retirement savings. Read the article below to learn more about IRAs.

Choosing the Right IRA

Often mistaken for a type of investment, IRAs are actually a type of account that you fund with your choice of investments. IRAs grow tax deferred, which means that you don't pay taxes on them while they are growing, so they grow faster. Everyone with earned income is eligible to set up an IRA, whether or not they have a retirement plan at work.

There are two basic types of IRAs: Traditional and Roth. Deciding which type of account to open can be a major decision since they are both great ways to save for retirement. However, they can have very different financial consequences both now and in the future. Here are some basics to help you decide which one to choose:

Traditional IRAs

- There are no income limits for eligibility. Anyone with earned income can set up a traditional IRA.
- Depending on your income and your eligibility to participate in an employer-sponsored retirement plan, your contributions may be tax deductible. In general, singles

Continued on the next page

with incomes of less than $65,000 and couples filing jointly with incomes of less than $109,000 are eligible to deduct their contributions. (**Note:** Income limits for couples increase to $176,000 if they are not eligible to participate in an employer-sponsored plan.)

- Contributions must stop at age 70 1/2.
- Withdrawals are required at age 70 1/2, and
- withdrawals before age 59 1/2 may incur a 10% penalty. Taxes are due in the year withdrawals are made.

Roth IRAs

- Eligibility to set up a Roth IRA is limited based on your income. Roth IRAs are available to single-filers earning less than $120,000 a year or couples earning less than $176,000 annually.
- You can make contributions beyond age 70½. However, your contributions are never tax deductible.
- There is no mandatory distribution age. Your contributions can remain in your account indefinitely.
- Principal contributions (money you put in) can be withdrawn at any time without penalty (subject to some minimal conditions).
- Withdrawals (including principal and earnings) are **100% tax free** if you follow the rules and regulations—a benefit that could mean thousands of dollars in future tax savings.

Choosing to invest in an IRA is not just a good idea; it can help your money grow faster, and save money on your taxes as well!

Note: Contribution limits for IRAs in 2012 is $5,000 and $6,000 for those over age 50. Get updates on annual contribution limits at www.squeezeyourmoney.com.

Hey, wait a minute. What are tax-deferred investments and are they better or worse than non-tax-deferred investments?

Good question, Harvey. Tax-deferred investments are investments that you don't have to pay tax on while they are growing, and, as a result, they grow faster. So I guess you could say they are better than non-tax-deferred investments. Typical tax-deferred investments include IRAs and employer-sponsored retirement plans like 401(k)s an 403(b)s. However, there is one thing to keep in mind. Although these investments grow tax-deferred, you may have to pay taxes on them when you take them out. *(See the example below to see how much faster they grow.)*

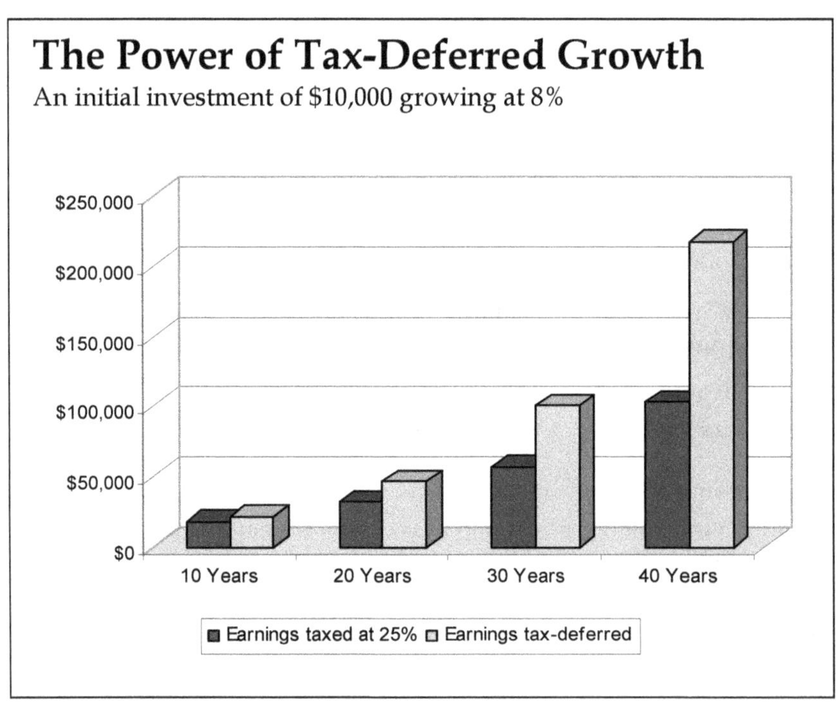

Four Strategies to Kick Start Your Investment Program

If you're feeling overwhelmed by all of the information in this chapter, and you aren't sure where to start, here's a four-step strategy to get you started:

1. Review your goals and choose one to start with. Determine the main objective or what you want your money to do. For example, do you want it to grow, to provide you with an income stream, or do you just want to keep it safe because you will need it soon?

2. Based on your objective select a basic investment category (cash, stocks, or bonds), and use the chart below to help guide you:

Preservation of Capital (Safety)	Income	Growth
Examples: Savings Accounts, CDs,[1] Money Market Accounts and Funds, and Treasury Bills	Examples: Bonds, Bond Mutual Funds, and ETFs	Examples: Stocks, Stock Mutual Funds, and ETFs

3. Review any current investments you have to see if you could add to one of them or reinvest the funds in something more appropriate for your goal. Use the investment pyramid on p. 186 to get more ideas of specific ideas of investments, and then conduct some research to narrow your search. Mutual funds are a good place to start so be sure to review p. 198 again regarding the five things you should know before choosing a mutual fund. If you have some time before you will

[1] Certificates of deposit

need the money and you want it to grow, why not simplify the process even more by starting with an index fund like one that tracks the S&P 500. Then once you're more comfortable with the process, you can branch out from there.

4. Finally, choose a company to work with, and make the call or go online and get started. I have listed some companies you can start with in the Resources & Terms at the end of this chapter, or if you are familiar with another company, contact it. In either case, don't wait any longer. The sooner you get started investing, the sooner you can start to build wealth!

Start Investing With Your Retirement Plan at Work

If you have a retirement plan at work such as a 401(k), 403(b), or 457 plan, that's a great place to get started investing, especially if you have a company match. Start by visiting one of the online calculators to develop a personalized asset-allocation model. Then review the options in your plan to see which ones will fit with your asset-allocation plan so you can build a diversified portfolio. If your choices include mutual funds, before you make your final selection, review the actual funds (the prospectus) and evaluate them using the criteria on pp. 198-200. Once you are satisfied that they fit with both your asset-allocation and your risk-tolerance, then sign up.

*(**Note:** Choosing the right investments for big goals like retirement is so important. If you're not sure, get some guidance from a financial professional. But don't just let them tell you what to do. Have them explain why, or better yet, have them teach you so you can do it yourself next time.)*

CASE STUDY: Emergency Fund Goal

George has a goal to accumulate $5,000 in an emergency fund so that he can stop relying on his credit cards everytime something comes up. Here is the investment plan George designed:

Goal: Accumulate $5,000 in an emergency fund.
Investment Plan:

- Have $150 a month automatically transferred from checking to a high-yield savings account like the one at ING Direct.
- When the account reaches a value of about $4,000, transfer $2,000 into a mutual fund with a higher yield and then have all future payments go into the mutual fund.

Note: Read more about George and see his overall plan on p.176.

RESOURCES & TERMS

Mutual Fund Companies and Brokers

Vanguard	800-992-8327	www.vanguard.com
E*Trade	800-387-2331	www.etrade.com
Fidelity	800-343-3548	www.fidelity.com
TD Ameritrade	800-454-9272	www.tdameritrade.com
Charles Schwab	866-232-9890	www.schwab.com
Ariel Investments	800-292-7435	www.arielinvestments.com
T. Rowe Price	800-638-5660	www.troweprice.com

High-Yield Savings

ING Direct	800-464-3473	www.ingdirect.com
Ally	877-247-2559	www.ally.com

SQUEEZE POINTS:

- ***Squeeze Principle #10: Investing is not just for the wealthy—it's also for those who want to get that way so get started sooner rather than later!***

- Before starting an investment program, consider the following:

    - All investments have risk, so be ready to accept that this is a part of investing.
    - The real purpose of investing is to fund your goals, so keep them in mind, along with your time frame as you develop your portfolio.
    - Start or have an emergency fund in place so that you can lessen the possibility that you will have to liquidate your long-term investments for daily emergencies once you get started.
    - Understand concepts like asset allocation and diversification to get the best returns while minimizing your risk.
    - Develop a discipline strategy so you stick with your program once you get started.

- While there are lots of different types of investments, they all tend to fall into three main categories: cash, stocks, and bonds.

- Basic investment definitions to understand:

    - Stocks represent part ownership in a company.

Continued on the next page

SQUEEZE INFO BLOCKS *(continued):*

- Bonds are loans or debt instruments.
- Mutual funds are a collection of investments. They can be all cash, stocks, bonds or a combination of these.
- ETFs (Exchange-Traded Funds) are a collection of investments similar to index mutual funds. However, unlike mutual funds, they are traded on the major exchanges like stocks.

▶ Risk and reward tend to move together. As the risk increases (or the potential to lose money), the higher the potential return.

SQUEEZE ACTION ITEMS:

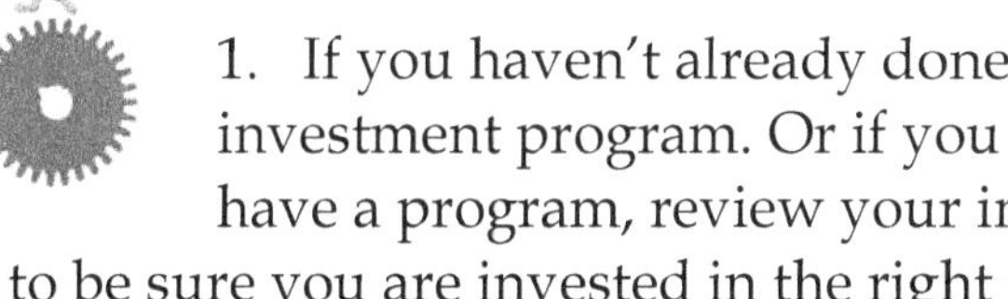

1. If you haven't already done so, start an investment program. Or if you already have a program, review your investments to be sure you are invested in the right types for the goals you want to achieve. Once you get started, use an asset-allocation model to build a complete portfolio.
2. Now that you understand the basics, complete any goals you listed in Chapter 12 that require investments.

SQUEEZE STORY:

Terry

I found what I thought was a guaranteed investment, so I withdrew money from my retirement plan to invest in it, and my intention was to put the money back within the 60-day window that the rules allow so I wouldn't have to pay taxes or a penalty. After all it was a sure thing with a quick turnaround. Well, I guess you know where I'm going with this...it turned out to not be such a sure thing. I lost most of my money, which means I may have to delay retirement for a year or two to make up for the lost money, plus I got hit with taxes and a 10 percent penalty, which I had to go in debt to pay. I can't believe this happened, and my wife didn't find out until we filed the taxes. Things are still a little strained at home.

SQUEEZE STORY UPDATE:

Kirsten

I'm so happy because I finally finished something that I started. We have a very knowledgeable personnel director who helped me set up my 401(k) and I'm making contributions up to the match of 6 percent. Also, I set up a Roth IRA and contributed the max for the year, and I'm saving for a down payment on a house. But the best news of all...I found Mr. Right...he's the personnel director at my new job!

(Read Kirsten's story on p. 32.)

CHAPTER FOURTEEN

MANAGING YOUR CREDIT LIFE

"Knowledge is the only instrument of production that is not subject to the law of diminishing returns."

– John Maurice Clark

"And the more you know about your credit life, the less it can be used against you!"

– Patricia Stallworth

Squeeze Principle #11: Your credit score can add/subtract thousands of dollars to/from your pockets over your lifetime. Always know yours and how it effects you in dollars and cents!

YOUR CREDIT LIFE CONSISTS OF THREE ELEMENTS: YOUR CREDIT SCORE, YOUR CREDIT REPORT, AND PROTECTING YOUR IDENTITY.

Managing your credit life is so important because it can benefit or hurt you in so many ways financially. In the past, things were a bit simpler, and your credit life only really mattered when you wanted to borrow money or get credit. But things have changed, and today it's not just lenders who make decisions about you based on your credit life. It's also insurance companies who charge you premiums based on it, landlords who decide whether or not to rent to you based on it, and some employers are also using it to decide whether or not to hire you. In other words, your credit life plays a central role in so many important areas of your life.

Your credit life consists of three basic elements: your credit score, your credit report, and protecting your identity. All of these affect the others, and if either one of these is incorrect or has been compromised, it could have disastrous effects for you. For example, according to information on the MyFico.com website, the difference in the interest rates offered to a person with a score of 620 and a person with a 720 score is 1.59 percentage points on a $200,000 30-year fixed mortgage.[1] That translates into approximately a $185 difference in monthly payments, and over the life of the loan could result in almost $68,000 in extra interest payments! So your credit life or in this case, one element, your credit score, can literally cost you thousands of extra dollars.

We will explore each element of your credit life along with suggestions on how you can maximize your credit life to *squeeze* the most out of what you have.

Keeping Tabs on Your Credit Score

Your credit score gives lenders a simple way to measure the likelihood that you will repay any loan or line of credit they extend to you, and so it is one of the first things they look at before making a decision. Credit scores range between 300 and 850, and the higher the

[1] Source: www.myfico.com February 2012. Note: As interest rates rise, the difference in rates/payments between high and low credit scores could also widen.

number, the better your chances of obtaining larger amounts of credit at lower interest rates or receiving better terms.

WHERE DOES YOUR CREDIT SCORE COME FROM?

Each of the three major credit bureaus—Equifax, Experian, and TransUnion—compiles a credit score, sometimes referred to as a FICO score, based on the information in you credit report (don't worry—more about that next). Your credit score is composed of five factors: your payment history, the amount you owe, the length of your credit history, new credit you apply for, and the types of credit you have. *(See the chart below.)*

Because each of the credit bureaus calculates your credit score using a different program, and lenders may only report information to one credit bureau (**Note:** They are not required to report any information), it's not unusual to have a different credit score at each credit bureau. That's why it's important to check your score at all three major credit bureaus before you apply for a loan, so can see what each one is reporting before a prospective lender.

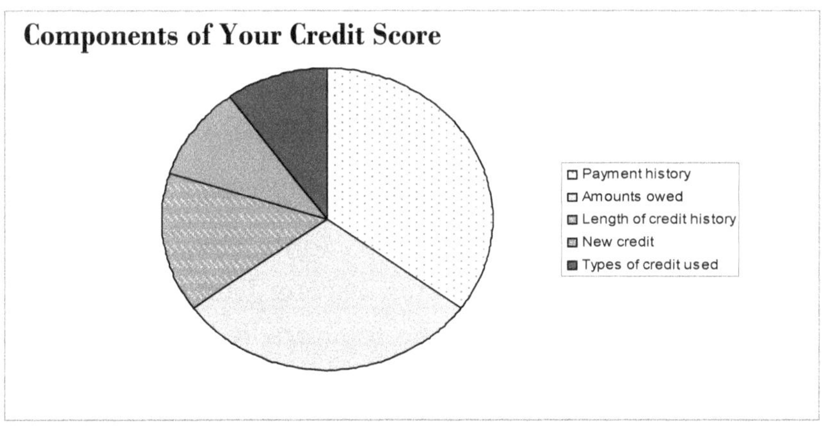

Payment History

Your payment history makes up approximately *35 percent* of your credit score. Information that makes up this part of your credit report is provided by creditors and collectors. The information is not confirmed by the bureaus; it is merely recorded.

YOUR PAYMENT HISTORY MAKES UP 35% OF YOUR CREDIT SCORE SO THE BEST WAY TO MAINTAIN OR BOOST YOUR SCORE IS TO PAY YOUR BILLS ON TIME.

Some of the factors that make up this component include:

- Payment information on credit cards, retail accounts, installment loans, and mortgage loans.
- Adverse public records, such as bankruptcy, judgments, liens, suits, wage attachments, and collection items.
- Delinquent accounts and collection items, and how long they have been past due. The longer it was past due, and the more recent it was, the more negative the impact on your score. For example, if you made a payment last month that was 60-days overdue, it will affect your credit score more than a payment that was 90-days late several years ago.
- The number of accounts paid as agreed.

Amounts Owed

The balances you owe on your accounts make up approximately *30 percent* of your credit score. Each account you have is weighted against the total credit line or limit of credit originally extended to you. Using 30 percent or less of your total credit line or limit is ideal. So if you have a total credit limit of $25,000 on all of your accounts, your ideal balances should total no more than $7,500, and some suggest that to boost your score, use an even lower amount such as 10 percent.

Some of the factors that make up this component include:

- The amounts you owe on specific types of accounts. For example, on loans like auto and mortgage loans, the current balance is compared to the original loan amount that remains constant. So a $20,000 auto loan that you owe $10,000 (50% of the original loan) on would be viewed more favorably than if you owed $18,000 (90% of the original loan) on that loan. And in the case of credit cards, the outstanding balance is weighed against the maximum amount of available credit. Again, ideally you should use no more than 30 percent of your available credit in all categories combined.

- The number of accounts with balances. The more accounts you have with balances, especially high ones, the more likely it is to reflect negatively on your credit score.

- How much of your total credit line is being used. If you're close to maxing out your credit cards and *revolving* accounts, it could be an indication you'll have trouble making future payments.

Length of Credit History

The length of your credit history makes up approximately

15 percent of your credit score. The longer your credit history, the better because lenders see this as an indicator of how stable you are. The length is determined two ways—how old your credit file is and the average length of time accounts have been in your credit file. The date opened determines the oldest account, and the average length is set by averaging the length of every account in your credit report. That's why it hurts your credit score when you cancel older credit cards, even though they may not have favorable rates or features for you. (**Note**: Interest rates are not a factor in calculating your credit score.)

New Credit

Applying for new lines of credit lines makes up approximately *10 percent* of your credit score. This includes the length of time since you opened an account and how many inquiries (or requests for new credit) have been made. It's the combination of applying for multiple accounts in a short period that has the greatest negative effect on your credit score.

However, the effect is not as great when shopping for a mortgage or a car loan if you do it in a relatively short period of time (less than 30 days). In this case, all of your inquiries are considered as one. The one caveat is that it having several lenders check your credit does have some effect, and it could be just enough to mean the difference between being offered the very best rate or a lower rate because the previous inquiries lowered your score slightly and pushed you down on the scale. For example, the difference between a 5.25 percent 30-year mortgage and a 5.5

percent 30-year mortgage on a $200,000 loan is about $31 a month. That's more than $370 a year and over the life your loan could add up to a substantial amount. So whenever possible, wait until you are sure you want to make a purchase from a specific lender before you allow them to check your credit.

Types of Credit Used

The different types of accounts you have—credit cards, retail accounts, installment loans, car loans, and mortgages—makes up approximately *10 percent* of your credit score. Having multiple types of accounts (installment, revolving, auto, mortgage, cards, etc.) is generally a good thing for your scores because it shows your ability to manage different account types. However, be aware that having too many accounts can be as detrimental as having too few, and if lenders feel you have too many open accounts already, they might be hesitant to extend any additional credit to you.

SO WHAT'S A GOOD CREDIT SCORE?

Credit scores range from 300 to 850 and scores above 700 are considered very good by most lenders because they are believed to represent a lower risk. Having a higher credit score not only saves you money, but you can often get better terms. On the other hand, you're considered a higher risk if you have a credit score below 600, and while you will most likely still be approved for a loan, you will, probably pay a higher interest rate and receive less-favorable terms.

FIVE STRATEGIES TO IMPROVE YOUR CREDIT SCORE

1. **Pay your bills on time**. The longer your history of paying your bills on time the better.
2. **Review your credit reports from all the three major credit bureaus and correct any errors immediately**. Do this at least once a year because errors can lower your score.
3. **Payoff your balances each month or keep a very low balance** on your credit cards and revolving debt.
4. **Be careful about moving debt from one account to another to get a lower rate, especially if you're opening and closing accounts.** Remember, opening accounts is a voluntary inquiry and closing accounts could shorten your credit history.
5. **Avoid signing up for credit if you don't really need it**. **Note:** Getting 10 percent off of your current purchases is usually not a good reason.

Shopping for a Mortgage or Car Loan? Here's a Strategy to Get the Best Rate…

Start by checking your credit reports from the three major credit bureaus, and correcting any errors. Once you are satisfied with your report, visit www.myfico.com to get an idea of the rates for loans with your credit score. Then shop around. If possible, make a decision in thirty days or less to minimize the damage to your credit score.

What's in Your Credit Report?

Your credit life is based on the information in your credit report, so it's important to understand what's in it. Although each credit-reporting agency formats and reports your information differently, all credit reports contain basically the same categories of information. For example, they all include:

- **Identifying information**. Information like your name, address, Social Security number, date of birth, and employment information are included to identify you. Identifying information is not used in credit scoring, and updates of this information comes from information you supply to lenders.
- **Credit trade lines.** These are your credit accounts. Lenders report on each account you have established with them. They report the following:
    - The type of account (bankcard, auto loan, mortgage, etc.)
    - The date you opened the account
    - Your credit limit or loan amount
    - The account balance
    - Your payment history
- **Credit inquiries.** An inquiry occurs when a lender requests a copy of your credit report. This section contains a list of everyone who accessed your credit report within the last two years. It includes both *voluntary* inquiries (when you apply for a loan) and *involuntary* inquires, like those made by lenders who send you pre-approved credit offers in the mail. *(**Note**: Only the*

voluntary inquiries affect your credit score.)

- **Public record and collection items.** Credit reporting agencies also collect public-record information from state and county courts, and information on overdue debt from collection agencies. Public record information includes bankruptcies, foreclosures, suits, wage attachments, liens, and judgments.

Everyone is entitled to receive a free copy of their credit report from each of the three major credit bureaus each year from www.annualcreditreport.com or by calling 877-FACTACT (1-877-322-8228). And it's a good idea to take advantage of this because it's estimated that 70 percent of all reports contain errors, and of those 25 percent are severe enough to cause you to either be denied credit or to receive less-than-favorable terms. Once you get your credit reports (and why not stagger them so you receive one every four months), review them thoroughly and dispute any errors. Errors can range from seemingly minor ones like the wrong address or employers on your file to credit accounts you never opened. I say "seemingly" because a wrong address could be a signal that identity thieves are rerouting your mail to cover their tracks, and wrong employers could signal that they have mixed your file with someone else's, so check every detail. *(**Note:** Credit bureaus have thirty days to either prove the information in dispute is valid or remove it.)*

Finally, given the importance attached to your credit report and the resulting credit score, it pays to be vigilant so be proactive in managing this vital area.

Dispute Credit Report Errors Immediately!

It's estimated that at least 70 percent of all credit reports have errors and of those 25 percent are severe enough to cause you to be denied credit or receive unfavorable terms. This is largely because credit bureaus do not check the information they receive—they simply report it.

Credit report errors can range from the wrong address to having the wrong accounts listed in your file, and every error should be taken seriously. For example, a wrong address could be a sign that identity thieves are diverting your information to a new address they have set up. And accounts that you did not set up could be a clerical error, or again, a sign that identity thieves are at work. And in the latter case this could result in higher rates or cause you to even be denied credit. Your best defense is to check your credit reports regularly and report any errors, no matter how minor they seem, immediately.

To report errors, contact the credit bureau that reported it. You can do this by filing a report on its website or by calling the bureau. *(See the Resources & Terms for contact information.)*

Hey, wait a minute. Instead of contacting the credit bureaus, can't I just use one of the credit repair services? They say they can get anything off my credit report.

Yes, but you should know that a credit repair service can't do anything more than you can. If something is wrong, you can follow a simple procedure to get it removed, and if something is correct, there is little you can do beyond negotiating a deal with your creditors or writing a letter of explanation and waiting until it is automatically scheduled to be deleted from your report.

RESOURCES & TERMS

- FICO - Fair Isaac Corporation www.myfico.com - get your credit scores and check general rates for loans on mortgages and cars based on your credit score. There is a fee for credit scores.

- Free annual credit reports: www.annualcreditreport.com or call 877-FACTACT.

- Contact information for the three major credit bureaus:

Experian - www.experian.com 888-397-3742
Equifax - www.equifax.com 800-685-1111
TransUnion - www.transunion.com 800-888-4213

Terms

revolving debt: The kind of debt that credit cards offer. It typically has a credit limit, a variable interest rate, and open-ended term and payments that are based on a percentage of the balance.

Be Proactive—Protect Your Identity!

Identity theft is one of the fastest-growing crimes in America, and it can happen to anyone. Sadly, it only takes identity thieves a fraction of the time to undo all of your efforts to create a good name and a good credit record, and it can take you months or even years to repair the damage. Being proactive—making it more difficult for thieves to get to you—is one of the best ways to protect your identity.

Identity thieves use a variety of sources to get your personal information and once they have it, they can use it to rack up huge amounts of debt, purchase large items like cars, or even file for bankruptcy or commit crimes using your name. Some common information-gathering sources used by identity thieves include:

- stealing information from businesses and institutions
- stealing your mail
- rummaging through your trash—"dumpster diving"
- gaining access to your credit report
- burglarizing your home or stealing your wallet or purse
- obtaining information from you by phone or the Internet

Identity thieves will either use your existing accounts to make purchases or they will use your Social Security or other information to open new accounts. If they use your existing accounts, you will most likely find out when you review your bank or credit card statements, or if you receive a call from your bank or credit card company wanting to verify a recent purchase. On the other hand, if they use your information to open new accounts, you may not find out until you check your credit report, receive a call from a creditor, or you are denied credit and you check to find out why. So reading your statements as soon as they arrive, and checking your credit reports periodically can help you catch things more quickly and possibly lessen the damage.

> READING YOUR STATEMENTS AS SOON AS THEY ARRIVE AND CHECKING YOUR CREDIT REPORTS PERIODICALLY CAN HELP YOU CATCH THINGS MORE QUICKLY AND POSSIBLEY LESSEN THE DAMAGE.

SEVEN STRATEGIES TO PREVENT IDENTITY THEFT

While you can't control all access to your information, there are some things you can do to make it more difficult for identity thieves to obtain and use your information. Here are seven strategies to help lesson your chances of becoming a victim of identity theft:

#1 Protect Your Financial Information.

- ***Protect your Social Security number (SSN).*** Your SSN is one of the most valuable pieces of information you have so take extra care to protect it. Don't carry it in your card in your purse or wallet, and never give it out unless it is absolutely necessary. The Federal Trade Commission suggests you ask the following questions before you give out your SSN:
    - Why do you need it?
    - How will it be used?
    - How do you protect if from being stolen?
    - What law says I must give it to you?
    - What will happen if I don't give it to you?
- ***Review your credit reports on a regular basis.*** Look for errors such as misspelled names, the wrong SSN, wrong addresses or employers, or new accounts or credit applications you did not authorize. (**Note:** Try staggering your free credit reports throughout the year so you can receive one every four months instead of getting all three at once so you can possibly find any discrepancies faster.)

#2 Secure Your Financial Information.

- ***Photocopy the contents of your wallet.*** Make a copy of your credit cards, driver's license, union cards, etc. (front and back), and place the copy in a safe place in your home. This will make reporting losses easier.

- ***Never include your driver's license number or SSN on checks***. That's just an open invitation for thieves.
- ***Treat your mail and trash with care.*** Regularly go through your mail. Separate out documents that include sensitive information and shred them. Sample documents to shred include: pay stubs, charge receipts, copies of credit applications, insurance forms, physician statements, checks and bank statements, expired charge cards, and credit offers you receive in the mail. In other words, shed anything that has personal information about you, even something as simple as an airline boarding pass. You would be surprised at how little information thieves need to get into your accounts.
- ***Do not mail bill payments and checks from home***. Always take them to the post office or use a secure mailbox.

#3 *Read Your Statements as Soon as They Arrive.*

Open your bank, credit card, and investment statements as soon as they arrive. Look for items you did not order or authorize. If you have authorized your credit card company to deduct payments from your bank account, be sure you request an email copy of your statement several days before the payment is deducted so that you can review it for accuracy. Most companies have a limit on the number of days you have to dispute a charge so allow yourself plenty of time. It could mean the difference between having a charge removed and having to live with it.

#4 Be Stingy with Your Personal Information.

- ***Don't give out personal information on the phone, in the mail, or on the Internet*** unless you've initiated the contact or you are sure you know who you are dealing with. Never respond to e-mails that look like they have been sent by the IRS, the Social Security Administration, other government agencies or banks that are requesting personal information. They will never ask for sensitive information by e-mail.
- ***Beware of revealing too much on social media and promotional sites.*** This is quickly becoming a haven for identity thieves so limit the amount of personal information you reveal. Virtual identity thieves can use this information to customize scams just for you, including impersonating a friend or family member and convincing you to give them personal financial data. You might even want to consider altering some of your personal information when registering at sites to further protect yourself. For example, instead of giving out your true birth date, give the year and substitute another month and date.

#5 Guard Your Passwords and PINs

- ***Memorize the passwords and/or PINs on your credit card, bank, and phone accounts.*** Avoid creating them using easily available information, such as your mother's maiden name, your birth date, the last four digits of your SSN or your phone number, or a series of consecutive numbers. And do not keep them in your wallet or out in the open. If you must keep a copy, find a safe place for it.

#6 Use Credit Cards, ATM or Debit Cards, and Checks with Care.

Using each of these can result in consequences relating to identity theft so be aware of the protections they offer and your responsibilities.

- *Credit cards* – If you report a lost or stolen card before the card is used, the credit card issuer cannot hold you responsible for any charges. If you report it within sixty days, and charges have already been made, you are responsible for $50. And you may also have the opportunity to dispute fraudulent charges before you pay the bill if it is beyond sixty days.
- *ATM or debit cards* –If you report your card lost or stolen before it is used, you can't be held responsible for any unauthorized purchases. If you make the report within two days of discovering the theft, you can be held responsible for up to $50 in losses. After sixty days your liability jumps to $500. If you fail to report unauthorized transactions within 60 days after your bank mails you the statement with the fraudulent transactions, you could lose all of the money in your account and be responsible for additional charges, including fees for bounced checks.
- *Checks* – Believe it or not, checks could actually be riskier than credit or debit cards. If thieves gain access to your account, a blank check, or even a used check they can use it to withdraw money from your account. And since the laws are not as clear regarding check fraud, banks have a lot of power in deciding the outcome. Even if the fraud wasn't your fault, you may still face fees for bounced checks, and your name maybe reported to the ChexSystems network, a national database that alerts banks and lenders that potential borrowers pose a credit

risk, and it may be difficult to open future accounts, get loans, or even rent an apartment.

Hey, wait a minute. So what should I use?

There is no easy answer. But remember, debit cards and checks tend to be riskier than credit cards. When you pay with a credit card you are essentially taking out a loan that you will be billed for in the future, while with debit cards and checks, the money comes directly from your bank account, and fraud issues could take some time to be resolved. On the other hand, there are limits and safeguards in place for credit cards. Ask your bank about their policies, so you can make an informed decision.

#7 Follow Safe Computer And Phone Practices.

Before giving out sensitive information over the Internet always look for signs that it is a secure site such as https, shttp, or a locked lock. Always use a firewall program, especially if you use a high-speed Internet connection like cable or DSL that leaves your computer connected to the internet 24/7, or disconnect your computer when you are not using the Internet in order to deter hackers or tracking programs. Also, since most cell phones today are actually mini-computers, use some of the same precautions, such as installing an anti-virus program, and beware of downloading free apps. Some are fine, but others can wreak havoc with your phone and even take over it and your information. Some other precautions to take include:

- Not opening or downloading files from strangers
- Destroying all of the data on your computer before discarding it or erasing all of the data on your cell phone before discarding or recycling it. *(**Note:** You can use the eraser at www.wirelessrecycling.com to delete the data and recycle your phone.)*

FIVE IMMEDIATE STEPS TO TAKE IF YOUR PERSONAL INFORMATION IS LOST OR STOLEN OR YOU SUSPECT YOU ARE A VICTIM OF IDENTITY THEFT

If you believe you are or could be a victim of identity theft, here are five immediate steps to follow:

1. Place a fraud alert on your credit reports, and review your credit reports.

Fraud alerts can help prevent an identity thief from opening any more accounts in your name. Contact the toll-free fraud number of any of the three consumer reporting companies to place a fraud alert on your credit report. You need to only contact one of the three companies to place an alert. The company you call is required to contact the other two, which will place an alert on their versions of your report, too. *(See the Resources & Terms for contact information.)*

Once you place the fraud alert in your file, get your credit reports, and review them carefully. Look for inquiries from companies you haven't contacted, accounts you didn't open, and debts on your accounts that you can't explain. Check that all of the information like your SSN, address(es), name or initials, and employers are correct. If you find fraudulent or inaccurate information, get it removed. Continue to check your credit reports periodically, to be sure nothing out of the ordinary shows up.

2. Close the accounts that you know, or believe, have been tampered with or opened fraudulently.

Call and speak with someone in the security or fraud department of each company. Follow up in writing, and include copies (NOT originals) of supporting documents. It's important to notify credit card companies and banks in writing. *(See a sample letter on p. 238.)* Send your letters by certified mail, return receipt requested, so you can document what the company received and when. Keep a file of your correspondence and enclosures.

If identity thieves have made charges or debits on your accounts, or on fraudulently opened accounts, ask the company for the forms to dispute those transactions. Once you have resolved your identity theft dispute with the company, ask for a letter stating that the company has closed the disputed accounts and has discharged the fraudulent debts. This letter is your best proof if errors relating to this account reappear on your credit report or you are contacted again about the fraudulent debt.
If you open new accounts with these companies, always use new passwords and PINs.

3. Visit the Federal Trade Commission (FTC) or the

***Squeeze* website to download a booklet with the FTC's ID Theft Affidavit and forms.**

Use the forms to file crime reports with the police and creditors. The booklet also includes more detailed information on identity theft. Visit the FTC at www.ftc.gov or www.consumer.gov/idtheft or *Squeeze* at www.squeezeyourmoney.com/idtheft.

4. File a report with your local police or the police in the community where the identity theft took place.

Then, get a copy of the police report, or at the very least, the number of the report. It can help you deal with creditors who need proof of the crime. If the police are reluctant to take your report, ask to file a "Miscellaneous Incidents" report, or try another jurisdiction, like your state police. You also can check with your state Attorney General's office to find out if state law requires the police to take reports for identity theft.

5. File a complaint with the Federal Trade Commission.

By sharing your identity theft complaint with the FTC, you will provide important information that can help law enforcement officials across the nation track down identity thieves and stop them. The FTC can refer victims' complaints to other government agencies and companies for further action, as well as investigate companies for violations of laws the agency enforces.

You can file a complaint online at www.ftc.gov/idtheft or

call the FTC's Identity Theft Hotline, toll-free: 1-877-IDTHEFT (438-4338); TTY: 1-866-653- 4261; or write: Identity Theft Clearinghouse, Federal Trade Commission, 600 Pennsylvania Avenue, NW, Washington, DC 20580.

Sample letter to send to creditors where fraudulent accounts were opened:

Business name
Address
City, state, zip code
Re: MaryJo Victim -- Account #123456

Dear Sir or Madam,

Please be advised that I am the victim of identity theft. Without my authorization or knowledge an account was opened with you in my name. Specifically **(state the details of the identity theft such as a credit card was obtained in my name).**

Please close this account immediately.

In accordance with my rights under FACT, I hereby request that you investigate this matter fully. Please also notify all the credit reporting agencies and remove any negative information pertaining to this account from my credit report. Please also forward a letter to me, confirming that this has been done and acknowledging that charges made to this account are fraudulent.

Thank you in advance for your cooperation in this matter.
I may be reached at 123-256-7890 or by email at mjvictim@abc.com

Sincerely,

MaryJo Victim

*FACT - The Federal Fair and Accurate Credit Transactions Act

RESOURCES & TERMS

- Initial Fraud Alerts:

An initial fraud alert (IFA) stays on your credit report for at least 90 days. You may ask that one be placed on your credit report if you suspect you have been, or are about to be, a victim of identity theft. An IFA is appropriate if your wallet has been stolen or if you've been taken in by a scam, such as a "phishing" scam that targets your personal information via email. When you place an IFA on your credit report, you are entitled to a free credit report from each of the three major credit bureaus.

- Equifax: 1-800-525-6285; www.equifax.com; P.O. Box 74024 Atlanta, GA 30374-0241
- Experian: 1-888-397-3742; www.experian.com; P.O. Box 9532, Allen, TX 75013
- TransUnion: 1-800-680-7289; www.transunion.com; Fraud Victim Assistance Division, P.O. Box 6790, Fullerton, CA 92834-6790

SQUEEZE POINTS:

- ***Squeeze Principle #11: Your credit score can add/subtract thousands of dollars to/from your pockets over your lifetime. Always know yours and how it effects you in dollars and cents!***
- Your credit life consists of three basic elements: your credit score, your credit report, and protecting your identity.
- Five elements make up your credit score: your payment history, the percentage of your available credit you are using, the length of your credit history, the

SQUEEZE POINTS *(continued):*

number of new credit accounts you apply for, and the types of credit accounts you have.

- Be proactive—protect your identity! Always open statements as soon as they arrive, check your credit reports periodically, and correct any errors immediately, no matter how small.
- Know your rights and the steps to follow if you become a victim of identity theft.

SQUEEZE ACTION ITEMS:

1. Get a copy of your credit report, and check it thoroughly. If you find any errors, dispute them immediately by filing a report on the credit bureau website or by calling them directly.
2. Visit www.myfico.com to determine the current interest rate you would be charged on an auto loan or mortgage based on your credit score. If you like what you see, you can stop there, but if you don't, revisit the Five Strategies to Improve Your Credit Score on p. 224 and look for things you can do to start improving your credit score. Next, create a plan and get started right away.

CHAPTER FIFTEEN

FORMULATING A GET-OUT-OF-DEBT PLAN

"When you find yourself in a hole, quit digging!"
– Unknown

"There is no shame in being in debt; the real shame is doing nothing to get out!"
– Patricia Stallworth

Squeeze Principle #12: Don't let debt determine your destiny. If you're in too deep, make a plan to get out. Every dollar spent on debt today is a dollar you don't have to enjoy or invest for tomorrow!

Credit and debt are as much a part of American life as apple pie. And debt, like apple pie, can make you very sick if you eat or bite off too much. If you're unsure if you have too much debt, take the debt quiz below. If you answer yes to any of the statements, it could be a signal that you have too much debt. ***(Hint:** Just because you can pay your bills each month doesn't mean that you don't have too much debt.)*

Quiz: Do You Have Too Much Debt?

Instructions: Answer each question. Then review your answers to determine if you have too much debt.

1. My current savings/investments equal less than six months living expenses?

   ❑ YES ❑ NO

2. I usually only make the minimum payment on my credit cards each month.

   ❑ YES ❑ NO

3. I have at least one credit card that is near, at, or over the credit limit.

   ❑ YES ❑ NO

4. I occasionally use a credit card to pay for necessary items (groceries, gas, etc.) and not just for convenience or to earn reward points.

   ❑ YES ❑ NO

5. I am currently using 30 percent or more of my total available credit limit.

   ❑ YES ❑ NO

6. My debt-to-income ratio is greater than 50 percent, including housing. *(**Note:** You can learn more about calculating your debt-to-income ratio on p 137.)*

   ❑ YES ❑ NO

7. I have been denied credit.

   ❑ YES ❑ NO

8. I lie to family and/or friends about my spending/debt/savings.

   ❑ YES ❑ NO

9. My credit card debt increases as my income increases.

   ❑ YES ❑ NO

Regardless of whether or not you are able to pay your bills each month, if you checked any YES boxes it could be a sign that you have too much debt and that you could benefit from a get out of debt plan. In either case, eliminating unnecessary debt will keep more money in your pockets so that you can do the things that matter the most to you.

The 7- Step Get-Out-of-Debt Plan

Debt is a trap that can keep you from ever achieving financial independence, because you are essentially mortgaging your future to pay for the present. That is, you are promising to pay for things you buy now with future money. And, if you keep up this trend, you will never break free of debt. The *Squeeze* 7-Step Program was designed to help you get out of debt and back on track to achieve your goals.

***Note**: For some people this section will be a great start, but it won't be the only help they need. For example, if you're in serious debt and you're unable to pay all of your necessary expenses each month, you may need to work with a financial counselor with expertise in the areas where you need help. Some suggestions are included in the Resources & Terms section of this chapter. Also, do not start this program if your job could be in jeopardy and you do not have an adequate emergency fund. Instead, pay the minimums on your debt and save as much as possible. Then start your get-out-debt program when things are more stable.*

Step 1: Stop charging!

If you're in debt, continuing to charge only puts you deeper in debt. Get rid of all but one or two cards that you use *only* for extreme emergencies. Do not carry credit cards in your purse or wallet. Instead, leave them in a safe place at home or in a safe-deposit box. If you have recurring payments, such as subscriptions or bills that you pay each month with your credit card, consider continuing to do so only if they are for things you really need and you can pay them off each month as a part of a spending plan so that you do not take on any more debt. Otherwise, cancel them or make other payment arrangements. The goal is to stop using credit because you can't get out if you keep getting in.

Hey, wait a minute. If I can't use my charge cards, what happens if I have a semi-emergency? Where's the money going to come from?

I'm not quite sure what a semi-emergency is, but you have several options. The first is your Flexible Spending Money (See Chapter 6). You should still add money to this spending category each month for expected and unexpected expenses.

The next option could be to use your savings. It would be ideal to have an emergency fund or savings of at least $1,000 before you start your debt payoff program. Also, the extra dollars you find in your spending plan *(see Step 3)* could do double duty if an emergency occurs. So instead of applying them to reduce your debt one month, you could use them for your emergency. And remember, that as you pay off debts you will have even more extra money available.

Step 2: Make a commitment to do what it takes to get out of debt.

If you really want to get out of debt, get really clear about it and your motives for wanting to do so. Then make a commitment to see it through. Getting out of debt is not always easy, and it can require some sacrifice and take years to accomplish. If you're not committed to seeing the process through, you could end up making your situation worse than when you started. Start by picturing the end goal and what your life will be like when you are debt free. Once you have this picture in your head, put it into words so you can refer back to it when things get tough.

You can greatly increase your chances of success, especially in the beginning by following a few simple rules:

1. *Understand the moods, sights, sounds, and smells that trigger your spending.* Then stay away from those things as much as possible until they no longer control you. However, if you do find yourself in a tempting situation, one trick is to stop and break the purchase down into the number of hours you would have to work to pay for it. For example, if you make $20 an hour and the shoes you want cost $160 that means that you would have to work eight hours to pay for the shoes. If you can't picture yourself working eight hours for them, walk away.
2. *Create guidelines to follow.* For example, if something costs more than $50, make it a rule that you have to wait twenty-four hours before you can buy it—sort of a self-imposed cooling-off period. Setting up a rule like this will allow you enough time to determine if you really

need or want it that badly. Also, consider keeping a diary of everything you spend at least for the first two weeks. And if you must spend beyond your plan, use cash.

3. *Develop a really clear idea of the difference between "wants" and "needs" and don't confuse the two.* For example, you need a way to get to work, and while you may want it, you don't need a $50,000 car to get there. If getting out of debt is really important to you, consider less expensive alternatives.

Step 3: Review your *Squeeze* Spending Plan and calculate the amount of money you have available to put toward your debts.

Take a long look at your spending plan and search for hidden pockets of money that you can put toward your debts. Question every expense from buying brand names at the grocery store, to dollars you normally spend on things that are not absolutely necessary, such as new clothes, gym memberships, cable, subscriptions, etc. Even small cutbacks can add up over time. For example, if you normally each lunch out each day, try brown bagging it three times a week—at $8 a day, that's almost $100 a month! Look everywhere for places to cutback or downsize, and if you have a spouse or kids, get them involved. It's difficult to make this work if everyone's not working together toward the same goal. ***Warning:*** *Do not just arbitrarily cut back on your Flexible Spending Money because a portion of it is for normal expenses that occur throughout the year. Without this cushion, you may have no recourse but to use credit cards to cover those expenses, and that could take you back to square one.*

Next, consider ways to increase your income, such as selling some of the stuff that got you in debt in the first place or taking on an extra job. Any extra income can go a long way in helping you get out of debt faster.

Finally, make changes to the appropriate worksheets in your spending plan, and calculate the amount of money you can reasonably put toward your debts each month. Then create a new category on your *Debit/Checks Worksheet* called Debt Payoff, and put this amount in that category so you don't spend it elsewhere *(see the sample below)*. And, you may also want to plan to allocate any extra money that comes in or is leftover during the month to this category as well.

Squeeze: Debits/Checks Worksheet

Instructions: List all of the recurring bills you pay with debits, checks, online, or with authorized withdrawals. Do not include credit card payments. Use the categories or rename them to fit your needs.

	NAME	MONTHLY PLAN	MONTHLY ACTUAL	DIFFERENCE	HOW OFTEN[1]	DUE DATE
☐	Rent/Mortgage					
☐	Car Payment					
☐	Cell Phone					
☐	Cable					
☐	Utilities					
☐	Gas					
☐	Electric					
☐	Church					
☐	Insurance					
☐	Car Insurance					
☐	Health Insurance					
☐	Prescriptions					
☐	DEBT PAYOFF					
☐						
☐						
	TOTAL					

[1] monthly, quarterly, annually, etc.

Step 4: Create a detailed picture of your current situation.

Develop a list that includes all of your debt, including the company name, the type of debt, account numbers, balances, interest rates, annual fees, customer service numbers, and notes about the debt. You can pull much of this information from your latest *Squeeze* Spending Plan worksheets, but also use this opportunity to get really familiar with your credit card statements and to connect them to your cards. For example, actually take out your credit card and sit it next to your statement. Circle the balance, the interest charged, and your last payment. Next, calculate how much of your payment went to reduce your outstanding balance (subtract the interest charged from your last payment) and write that number next to the interest charged (it's probably a much smaller number). Repeat this exercise for each card so that you get the connection between the card and the statement. Once you understand how much you owe, how payments are applied, and the amount of interest you are paying (or throwing away) each month, complete the *Debt Summary Worksheet* on the next page.

Step 5: Negotiate with your creditors.

A surprising number of creditors are willing to reduce payments, extend the time to pay, drop late fees, reduce your rates or make other adjustments (temporarily or permanently). But they won't if you don't ask, so make the call.

Getting your rate lowered or getting any late or annual

Squeeze: Debt Summary Worksheet

Name of Company	Type of Debt*	Account Number	Balance	Interest Rate	Annual Fee	Customer Service #	Notes
Total							

* list your debt type like credit card, auto, mortgage, loan, etc.

fees dropped would be helpful, so focus on those areas when you make the call. Once you have a clear picture of what would help you the most, call customer service and ask for the change(s) you want. Remind them that you have been a loyal customer who has paid on time and that you want to stay with them, but you have offers from other companies at a lower rate (if it's true), and ask if they will lower your rate.

In lieu of making the changes you request, some companies will offer to put you on a payment plan. This generally includes a lower interest rate and is designed so that the card will be paid off in a set period of time. The catch is that they also usually cancel the card at the same time, which is not all bad. If this option is offered to you, try to get them to agree to close the account as closed by "consumer," not the creditor—and if they agree, get this in writing before you agree. The difference can mean several points on your credit report. However, if they won't agree, and you are in a real bind and this option helps, don't be foolish. You can always rebuild your credit score later.

On the other hand, despite your best efforts, some creditors will not budge. If this happens, don't take it personally. That's just the way they do business. Don't dwell on it. Just continue to plan your payoff strategy.

Step 6: Decide on a debt-payoff strategy.

The best way to attack debt is one at a time so instead of putting a little extra money toward each debt each month, develop a plan to pay them off one at a time. This will make the process easier, and it will take less time to reach your goal. Here are two basic tried-and-true strategies:

Option 1: Attack the debt with the lowest balance first. With this strategy, you pay the minimum payment on all of your debts, and then you put all of the extra money you have toward the debt with the lowest balance. This option tends to give you a psychological advantage because you get to see results faster, and this can motivate you to keep going. *(See the Smith Case Study on the next page.)*

Option 2: Attack the debt with the highest interest rate first. Again, make the minimum payments on all your debts. Then pay them off in order from the highest interest rate to the lowest. While this option does not have the same psychological advantage as Option 1, it usually results in paying less interest overall. *(See the Smith Case Study on the next page for a comparison of the two options.)*

Not sure which option to choose? Here's a suggestion to get the best of both options: Start with Option 1 or the lowest balance so can get an early taste of victory and then switch to Option 2 to pay off the remaining debts so the process can go faster and cost you less.

Once you decide on a strategy, complete the *Debt Planning and Payoff Worksheets* on pp. 256—257, including the amount of money you have available and the projected payoff date for each debt based on the payoff strategy you select. *(See the examples on pp. 252 – 255).*

Hey, wait a minute. Isn't it better to pay extra on all of the debts? I've always been told to get out of debt, always pay more than the minimum.

Continued on the next page

Harvey's Question *(continued)*

You're right, Harvey. However, when you have several debts that you want to pay off generally, the most efficient way is to attack them one at a time. Otherwise, the process can take a lot longer and result in you paying more in interest. Review the Smith's Case Study below to get a better idea of how these strategies work.

CASE STUDY: The Smith's Get-Out-of-Debt Plan

The Ed and Sharon Smith have decided to start a debt-reduction program and they want to be totally debt-free. After reviewing their spending plan and making some cuts, they found a total of $350 they can use each month to put toward paying off their debts.

Here are the details of their case:

Debt	Current Balance	Monthly Payment	Interest Rate
Credit card 1	$ 1,116	$ 45	20.00
Credit card 2	5,822	233	18.00
Credit card 3	3,220	129	26.00
Ed's car	17,745	502	8.00
Sharon's car	15,248	387	8.00
Mortgage	197,821	1,446	7.25

CASE STUDY: The Smith's Get-Out-of-Debt Plan *(continued)*

If the Smith's choose **Option 1** (the lowest balance first), their payoff plan would look like this:

#	Debt	Current Balance	Monthly Payment	Interest Rate
1	Credit card 1	$ 1,116	$ 45	20.00
2	Credit card 3	3,220	129	26.00
3	Credit card 2	5,822	233	18.00
4	Sharon's car	15,248	387	8.00
5	Ed's car	17,745	502	8.00
6	Mortgage	197,821	1,446	7.25

And they would payoff their first debt in approximately three months! [$350 + 45 = $395 $1116 ÷ $395 = 2.83 or 3 months] Then in month 4, instead of $350, they could apply a total of $524 [$350 + $45 + $129] to payoff their next debt (#2) since debt #1 would no longer exist. A real snowball effect would start and grow as they payoff each debt and free up more money to put toward the next one.

Calculate Your Target Payoff Dates

Use one of the online calculators, like the one at www.dinkytown.com, to calculate how long it will take you to pay off each card with the amount of money you have available to pay it off. Don't forget to increase the amount available after you pay off each debt.

CASE STUDY: The Smith's Get-Out-of-Debt Plan *(continued)*

On the other hand, if the Smith's choose **Option 2** (the highest interest rate first), their payoff plan would look like this:

#	Debt	Current Balance	Monthly Payment	Interest Rate
1	Credit card 3	$ 3,139	$ 129	26.00%
2	Credit card 1	1,116	45	20.00
3	Credit card 2	5,822	233	18.00
4	Ed's car	17,745	502	8.00
5	Sharon's car	15,248	387	8.00
6	Mortgage	197,821	1,446	7.25

And they would payoff their first debt in approximately seven months! [$350 + 129 = $479 $3,139 ÷ $479 = 6.6 months] Then instead of $350, they could apply a total of $524 [$350 + $129 + 45] to payoff their next debt (#2) since debt #1 would no longer exist. And again, the snowball effect would start to grow as they paid off each debt and freed up more money to put toward the next one.

Or to get the best of both worlds, the Smith's could start with **Option 1** and payoff their lowest balance debt first ($1,116), taste the victory in three months, and then move to **Option 2** to payoff their remaining debts. However, regardless of the method they choose, the important thing is to get started as soon as possible. See how it all works out for the Smith's on the next page.

CASE STUDY: The Smith's Get-Out-of-Debt Plan *(continued)*

Solution:

The Smith's decided to use **Option 2** (paying off the highest interest rate first) along with the additional $350 they found in their monthly spending plan. The Smith's paid off their debts in less than nine years and saved more than $147,000 in interest payments. Here's how they did it:

Debt	Current Balance	Interest Rate	Minimum Monthly Payment	Payoff Monthly Payment	# of Months to Payoff	Debt Paid In*
CC 3	$ 3,139	26.00%	$ 129	$479 starts in month 1	6.55	7 months
CC 1	1,116	20.00%	45	$524 starts in month 8	2.13	10 months
CC 2	5,822	18.00%	233	$757 starts in month 11	7.69	18 months
Ed's Car	17,745	8.00%	502	$1,259 starts in month 19	14.09	33 months
Sharon's Car	15,248	8.00%	387	$1,646 starts in month 34	9.26	43 months
Home Loan	197,821	7.25%	1,446	$3,092 starts in month 44	63.98	107 months

* All partial months were rounded to the next highest month.

Crafting Your Debt Payoff Plan

To get started, compete the *Debt Summary Worksheet* on p. 249. This will provide you with a list of all of your debts. Then transfer those debts you would like to payoff to the *Debt Planning Worksheet* below. Next, choose a strategy to pay off your debts (lowest balance first or highest interest rate). Finally, transfer the information from the *Debt Planning Worksheet* to the *Debt Payoff Worksheet* on the next page in the order you plan to pay them off and, using the example on p. 255, calculate the number of months to pay each debt off and the actual payoff date.

Squeeze: Debt Planning Worksheet

Instructions: List all of the debts you want to payoff. Include the name, balance, interest rate, the bill due date, and the minimum payment.

Name	BALANCE	INTEREST RATE	DUE DATE	MINIMUM PAYMENT
exp. VISA	*5,000*	*17.9*	*15*	*125*
TOTAL				

OPTION: ❑ Lowest balance ❑ Highest interest rate ❑ Combination

Monthly amount available to pay off debts: ______________

Squeeze: Debt Payoff Worksheet

#	Debt	Account Number	Current Balance	Interest Rate	Minimum Payment	Payoff Monthly Payment	# of Months to Payoff*	Payoff Date Month/Year
	Total							

* round all partial months to the next highest month

Step 7: Implement your plan and monitor your progress.

Your next step is to implement your plan—to follow the payoff plan you outlined on your *Debt Payoff Worksheet* and then to monitor your progress. As you payoff each debt, scratch it off the list, celebrate, and move to the next one. Each time you start paying off a new debt, recalculate the amount money you have available to pay it off and amount of time it will take you to pay it off based on the current balance pay.

RESOURCES & TERMS

- Resources for debt counselors: Look for non-profit organizations like the National Foundation for Credit Counseling (NFCC) at www.nfcc.org or call 800-388-2227. Also, CredAbility at www.credability.org

- Snowball Debt Elimination Calculator: www.dinkytown.com in the Credit Cards & Debt Calculators

SQUEEZE POINTS:

- ***Squeeze Principle #12: Don't let debt determine your destiny. If you're in too deep, make a plan to get out. Every dollar spent on debt today is a dollar you don't have to enjoy or invest for tomorrow!***

- Develop a plan to attack your debt. The Squeeze 7-Step plan includes the following steps:

    1. Stop charging—you can't get out of debt if you keep getting in.

SQUEEZE POINTS *(continued):*

2. Make a commitment to do what it takes to get out of debt. Even the best plan is doomed to fail if you are not really committed to it.
3. Calculate the amount of money you have available to put toward your debt.
4. Create a detailed picture of your current situation.
5. Negotiate with your creditors to see if they will lower your rate or drop late or annual fees.
6. Decide on a debt payoff strategy.
7. Implement and monitor. Even the best plan is of little use if you put it into action and monitor it to make sure you stay on track.

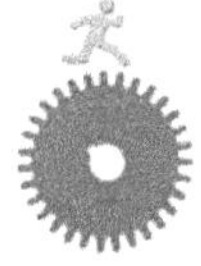

SQUEEZE ACTION ITEMS:

1. Calculate the amount of money you are spending on interest alone each month and if you don't like what you see, use the seven steps in the Squeeze Get-Out-of-Debt plan to pay off your debts.

   Additional worksheets are available at www.squeezeyourmoney.com.
2. Implement your plan and monitor your progress.

SQUEEZE STORY:

Susan

Shopping has always been second nature to be. I grew up shopping with my mother and I have never stopped. I don't always have the money so I started using credit cards. The minimum payments are reasonable so I saw no reason to stop using them. Then Tom proposed. I decided that honesty was the best policy but I wanted to know how bad it was before I talked to Tom. I don't know what I was thinking, but I certainly wasn't thinking the $57,642.37 that it turned out to be. I had no idea it was that bad. I couldn't tell that to Tom. So I scheduled an appointment with a credit counselor who set up a payment plan that I could do but it would take years and I didn't want to start a new marriage with such a big debt. Then I went to see a bankruptcy attorney but I found out that with the new bankruptcy laws, it wasn't going to work for me. Then in a flash of brilliance or conscious I decided to just tell the truth and let the chips fall where they may. WOW! What a guy I got. He wasn't overjoyed but he didn't think it was the end of the world either and we're going to work together to get rid of it as quickly as possible. In the meantime, I'm going cold turkey. I've cut up all of my cards except for one for emergencies which I put in a metal bowl of water and stuck in the freezer so when temptation comes along I can't do anything about it until the ice thaws. Hopefully, that will be enough time to come to my senses.

CHAPTER SIXTEEN

NEXT STEPS

"If you want to know your past life, look into your present condition;
If you want to know your future, look into your present action."

—Padmisabba

"So, in other words, what you make of your future is up to you!"

—Patricia Stallworth

I decided to open and close *Squeeze* with the same quotation because it seemed so appropriate for both places. You are the result of all of the things you have done up until now, and your future will be determined by the things you do now and going forward.

So What's Next?

Squeeze is all about getting the most out of every dollar on the surface, but underneath it's really about a building a lifestyle that includes consciously managing your money on a regular basis. Don't get caught in the old trap of believing that if you have to manage your money there must be something wrong. There isn't. Managing your money leads to something right and it's essential to making it work for you. Building wealth and a secure financial future don't just happen automatically, it requires input from you. In other words, your money needs your guidance to create a secure financial future for you.

A Place to Start

There's so much information in this book, it's easy to get overwhelmed so start with the basics first and then move on to other things. At the foundation of managing your money or *squeezing* back is knowing what's coming in, what's going out, and where it's going, and a *Squeeze Spending Plan* can answer all of those questions and more. So, if you don't have one, start a spending plan right away. Visit the *Squeeze* website[1] and use the password '**squeeze123**' to download all of the worksheets to complete your plan. Then review chapters 2–9 for a step-by-step guide to setup and maintain your spending plan.

Once you have a basic spending plan that works for you, you can begin to work on the *Squeeze Action Strategies* (SAS). Depending on your goals and concerns, you may not need to complete all of the action strategies. The charts on the next few pages summarize how the different action strategies interact and work together. In some cases, they provide vital information to complete another strategy and will need to be completed first while in other cases, they serve in a reporting, measuring, or monitoring capacity and you may need a before and after snapshot to truly measure your progress. For example, tracking your information *(Chapter 11)* will be needed for Step 1 of creating a financial game plan *(Chapter 12)* so complete it before you

[1] Download the worksheets at www.squeezeyourmoney.com/store using the password: **squeeze123**

start building a financial plan. And tracking your information *(Chapter 11)* is also needed before, during, and after to monitor your progress when working on a get-out-of-debt plan *(Chapter 15)*.

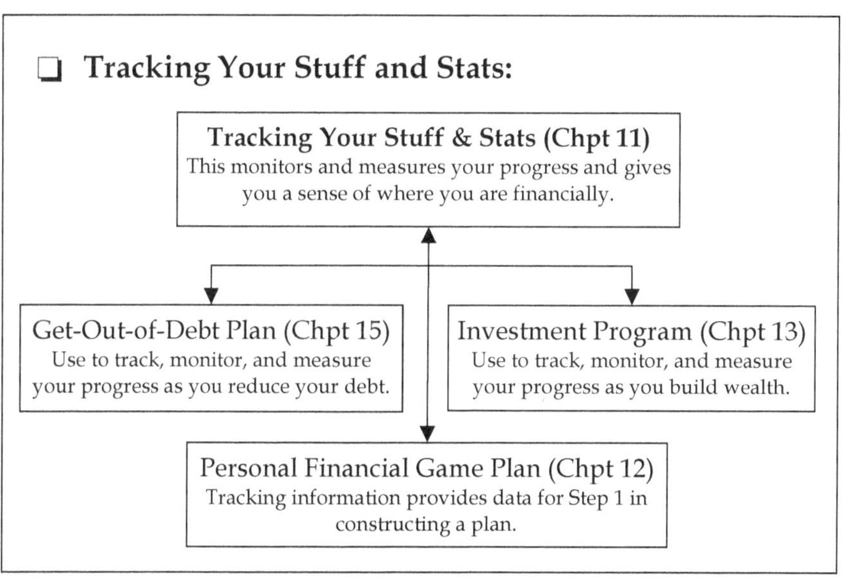

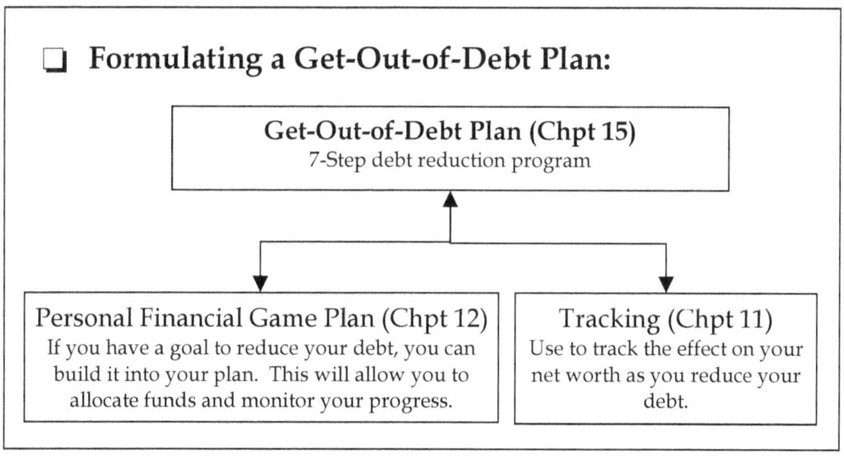

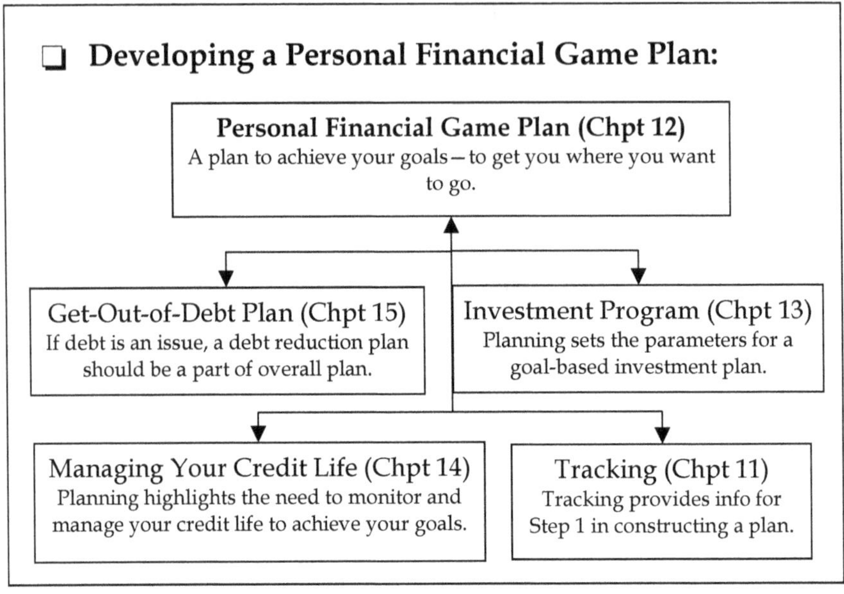
❑ Developing a Personal Financial Game Plan:
Personal Financial Game Plan (Chpt 12)
A plan to achieve your goals—to get you where you want to go.
Get-Out-of-Debt Plan (Chpt 15)
If debt is an issue, a debt reduction plan should be a part of overall plan.
Investment Program (Chpt 13)
Planning sets the parameters for a goal-based investment plan.
Managing Your Credit Life (Chpt 14)
Planning highlights the need to monitor and manage your credit life to achieve your goals.
Tracking (Chpt 11)
Tracking provides info for Step 1 in constructing a plan.

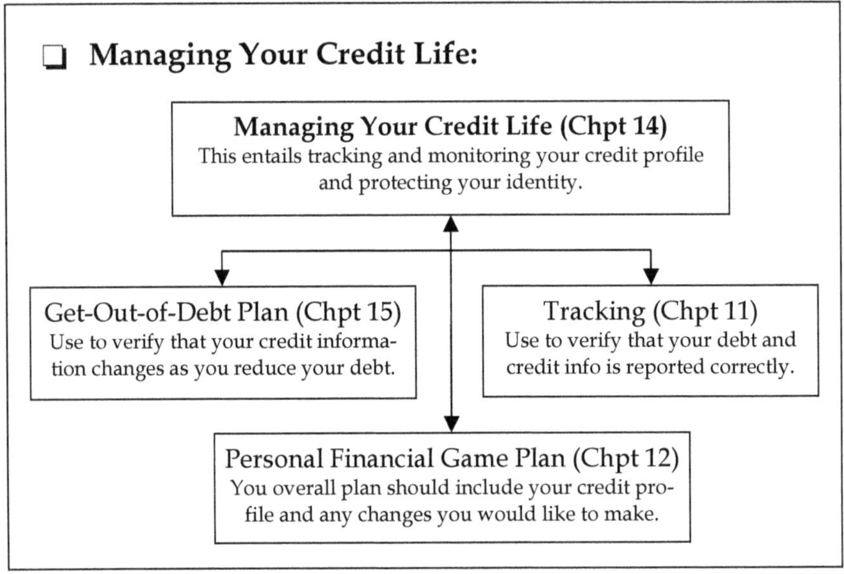
❑ Managing Your Credit Life:
Managing Your Credit Life (Chpt 14)
This entails tracking and monitoring your credit profile and protecting your identity.
Get-Out-of-Debt Plan (Chpt 15)
Use to verify that your credit information changes as you reduce your debt.
Tracking (Chpt 11)
Use to verify that your debt and credit info is reported correctly.
Personal Financial Game Plan (Chpt 12)
You overall plan should include your credit profile and any changes you would like to make.

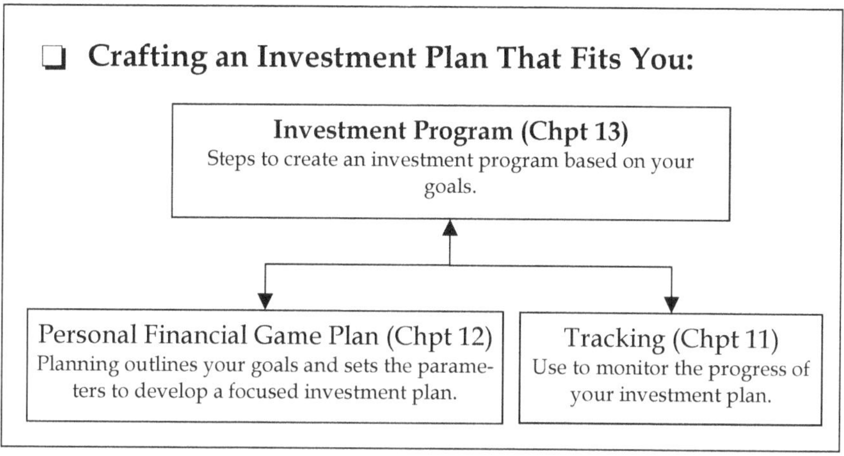

10 Sure Signs You're Squeezing Back

I started Squeeze with *10 Sure Signs You're Being Squeezed by Your Money* and if you saw yourself in any of those signs, hopefully that has changed or will change as you complete some of the exercises in *Squeeze*. As you implement some of the *squeeze* strategies it's a good idea to monitor your progress. Here's a quick quiz to help you keep track. Revisit it once a year to see how you're doing. Each question is worth one point and every time you answer TRUE, give yourself a point. See how close you can get to a perfect score!

1. I do not live paycheck to paycheck. I have a spending plan in place and I often have money left over to save or spend anyway I like.

   ❑ TRUE ❑ FALSE

2. I realize that my credit limit is not my money but rented money and I am working on or have my credit under control to the point that I can pay the bill off each month.

   ❑ TRUE ❑ FALSE

3. I have adjusted my tax withholding so that I do not get a large refund each year because a large refund is a signal that I am giving Uncle Sam an interest-free loan.

   ❑ TRUE ❑ FALSE

4. I open my bank and credit card statements soon after they arrive so that I can verify that the charges are correct and that I have been given credit for deposits and payments.

   ❑ TRUE ❑ FALSE

5. I have a savings program that I contribute to each month and I have an emergency fund that covers at least three-month's expenses.

   ❑ TRUE ❑ FALSE

6. I know how much my monthly bills are and the total amount of debt I have.

   ❑ TRUE ❑ FALSE

7. I have an investment program that I contribute to each month so that if an opportunity comes up or if I need to make a change in my life/relationship/job/location I have funds available so that I have a

great deal of flexibility.

❑ TRUE ❑ FALSE

8. I spend less than 30 percent of my gross income on housing expenses and all of my expenses total less than 70 percent of my income.

   ❑ TRUE ❑ FALSE

9. I proactively manage my credit life. I check my credit reports at least annually, correct any errors immediately, and I know my credit score.

   ❑ TRUE ❑ FALSE

10. I know what's coming in, what's going out, and where it's going each month and I regularly compare my spending projections to what actually happened so I also know my current financial situation.

    ❑ TRUE ❑ FALSE

BONUS

I know the best kept secret about money—that it's not good at managing itself—so I don't let it. This allows me to stay in control, to *squeeze* the most out of every dollar, and spend my money in ways to achieve my goals, including the fun ones.

❑ TRUE ❑ FALSE

Score: ______________ Date: ______________

Squeeze Epilogue

That's it, the entire *Squeeze Your Money System!* If there's one point I'd like to leave you with it's that there's only an upside to *squeezing* your money. It can help you to go from "have not" to "have" or "have more" as soon as you get serious about managing your money.

Finally, *Squeeze* is a marathon, not a sprint, so remember to celebrate your successes along the way. Sometimes we're so focused on getting to the finish line that we forget to enjoy the journey. Make it a point to stop and celebrate your successes after you complete a new plan, a goal, overcome an obstacle, or simply live to see a new dawn. Success breeds success, so celebrate each one!

Please let me know how you're doing and if you have questions or want to share a *Squeeze* story, contact me at ps@squeezeyourmoney.com. ps!

APPENDIX A

FINANCIAL INVENTORY

SQUEEZE: FINANCIAL INVENTORY

1. PERSONAL INVESTMENTS *(do not include retirement accounts)*

Cash

	Name of Bank / Institution	Type of Account	Current Balance	Interest Rate
	Example: Bank of North	*Checking/Savings/Money Market*	*$10,000.00*	*2%*
1.				
2.				
3.				
4.				
	Total Cash Reserves			

Fixed Income

	List Fixed Income Investments	Dollar Amount	Current %	Maturity Date
	Example: CD, Treasury Bills, Notes, Bonds, Tax-Free, Series EE Savings Bonds			

1.				
2.				
3.				
4.				
	Total Fixed Income			

Stocks

	Name of Company	**Number of Shares**	**Purchase Price**	**Date Purchased**	**Approximate Market Value**
1.					
2.					
3.					
4.					
	Total Stocks				

Do you have stock certificates in a safe-deposit box? ❑ Yes ❑ No

Name of bank ____________________ Address ____________________ Phone # ____________

Mutual Funds and/or Brokerage Accounts

	Name of Brokerage Firm / Mutual Fund	Number of Shares	Cost Basis	Date Purchased	Approximate Market Value
1.					
2.					
3.					
4.					
	Total Mutual Funds /Brokerage Accts				

Annuities

	Company	Annuitant/ Owner	Interest Rate	Date Purchased	Approximate Market Value
1.					
2.					
3.					
	Total Annuities				

Personal Loans *(loans you made to others)*

	Name	Relationship	Phone #	When Due?	Total Outstanding
1.					
2.					
	Total Personal Loans				

Other Assets *(e.g. Business Ownership, etc)*

	Name	Approximate Market Value
1.		
2.		
3.		
4.		
5.		
	Total Other Assets	

2. RETIREMENT ACCOUNTS

Employer-Sponsored Retirement Plans

	Name of Company Where Money Is	Type of Plan	Approximate Value	% You Contribute
	You:			
1.				
2.				
	Spouse:			
1.				
2.				
	Total Employer-Sponsored Retirement Plans			

Do you have money sitting in a company plan where you no longer work?

You: ❑ Yes ❑ No Balance ________ When did you leave the company? ________

Spouse: ❑ Yes ❑ No Balance ________ When did you leave the company? ________

Self-Directed Retirement Plans

Are you participating in a self-directed retirement plan? These include IRAs, Roth IRAs, SEP-IRAs, SAR-SEP IRAs, and SIMPLE Plans

	Name of Company Where Money Is	**Type of Plan**	**Approximate Value**
	You:		
1.			
2.			
	Spouse:		
1.			
2.			
	Total Self-Directed Retirement Plans		
	Total Employer-Sponsored Retirement Plans		
	Total All Retirement Plans	*(Employer + Self-Directed)*	

3. REAL ESTATE

Do you rent or own your home?

❑ Own Monthly Mortgage Payment ____________

Approximate Value of Primary Home $ ____________

– Mortgage Balance $ ____________

= Equity in Home $ ____________

❑ Rent Monthly Rent ____________

Do you own a second home? ________

Monthly Mortgage Payment ____________

Approximate Value of Primary Home $ ____________

– Mortgage Balance $ ____________

= Equity in Home $ ____________

Do you own any other real estate? ___________

Monthly Mortgage Payment _______________

Approximate Value of Primary Home $ _________________

− Mortgage Balance $ _________________

= Equity in Home $ _________________

Total Equity in Real Estate $ _________________

4. LIABILITIES

	Mortgage Company Name	Original Purchase Price	Current Loan Balance	Interest Rate	Fixed or Variable Rate?	Original Term of Loan	Remain-ing Time on Loan
1.							
2.							
3.							
	Total Mortgages/Home Loans						

Car/Boat Loans

	Vehicle	Lender/Institution	Current Balance	Interest Rate	Number of Months Remaining	Account Number	Phone Number
1.							
2.							
3.							
	Total Car/Boat Loans						

Credit Card Debt

	Name of Card/Company	Account Number	Current Balance	Interest Rate	Phone Number	Pin/ Password
1.						
2.						
3.						
4.						
5.						
6.						

7.						
8.						
	Total Credit Card Debt					

Student Loans

	School/University or Other Lender	Account Number	Current Balance	Interest Rate	Phone Number	Pin/ Pass-word
1.						
2.						
3.						
	Total Student Loans					

Personal Loans *(from a bank or individual)*

	Name/Institution	Balance Owed	Interest Rate	Phone Number	Date Due
1.					
2.					
	Total Personal Loans				

All Other Debt *(i.e. IRS, unpaid or overdue bills, outstanding contracts, etc)*

	Company/Expense	Balance Owed	Interest or Penalties	Date Due
	Example: Bob's Construction/kitchen remodel	*$5,000*	*n/a*	*7/11*
1.				
2.				
3.				
	Total Other Debt			

5. ESTATE PLANNING

Do you have a Will or Living Trust in place? ❑ Yes ❑ No

Date it was last reviewed? ________________

Who helped you create it? (Attorney's Name) ______________________________

Address ________________________ Phone Number ______________ Fax ______________

Is your home held in the Trust or is it held in Joint or Community Property? ________________

Do have a Power of Attorney or a Durable Power of Attorney? ❑ Yes ❑ No

Who is the person named to take over if you are unable to: ________________________

Do you have a Living Will or Health Directive? ❑ Yes ❑ No

	Life Insurance Company	**Type of Insurance** *(Whole Life, Term, Variable)*	**Death Benefit**	**Cash Value**	**Annual Premium**
1.					
2.					
3.					
	Total Insurance Cash Value				

Do you have Short-Term Disability Insurance? ❑ Yes ❑ No Percent of income replacement ______
# of days before benefits start ______ # of days benefits last ______ Premium ______

Do you have Long-Term Disability Insurance? ❑ Yes ❑ No Percent of income replacement ______
# of days before benefits start ______ # of days benefits last ______ Premium ______

Tax Planning

Do you have your Taxes professionally prepared? ☐ Yes ☐ No

Name of CPA/Preparer ____________________

Address ____________________ Phone Number ____________ Fax ____________

What was your Taxable Income last year? ____________

What is your estimated tax bracket? ________

Summary Notes:

Instructions: Place the totals from the *Financial Inventory Worksheet (see Appendix A)* in the appropriate categories. Total each section and then subtract your assets from your liabilities to calculate your net worth. Next project an amount or percent to increase your net worth in one, three, and seven years.

STATEMENT OF NET WORTH ____________
Date

Assets

Total Cash $ ____________
Total Fixed Income $ ____________
Total Stocks $ ____________
Total Mutual Funds $ ____________
Total Annuities $ ____________
Total Other Assets $ ____________
Total Retirement Accounts $ ____________
Total Real Estate $ ____________
Total Assets $ ____________

Liabilities

Total Mortgages $ ____________
Total Car/Boat Loans$ ____________
Total Credit Card Debt $ ____________
Total Student Loans $ ____________
Total Personal Loans$ ____________
Total All Other Debt $ ____________
Total Liabilities $ ____________

Net Worth

Total Assets $ ____________
– Total Liabilities – $ ____________
Estimated Net Worth $ ____________

Goal for Net Worth in:

1-Year ________ 3-Years _________ 7-Years _________

Signed: ____________________________ Date:____________

Signed: ____________________________

INDEX

HOW TO REACH US

...GO TO SQUEEZEYOURMONEY.COM

If you would like more information about *Squeeze* or workshops and classes taught by Patricia as well other financial education tools and services we offer, please visit our website at www.squeezeyourmoney.com.

Also, if this book has made an impact on you, I would love to hear from you. If you send me an e-mail with your success stories, ideas, suggestions, and/or questions to info@squeezeyourmoney.com, I promise I will read it.

ps!

Follow me: Twitter.com/PatStallworth
Linkedin.com/PatriciaStallworth
Facebook.com/SqueezeYourMoney

ABOUT THE AUTHOR

Patricia Stallworth is a speaker, an educator, and a 16-year veteran in the financial planning industry. She is the founder and CEO of PS Worth, a financial education and consulting firm whose mission is to arm women and men with the skills and tools to confidently take charge of their financial lives. And she is the author of several books, including *Minding Your Money* and *The 57 Most Frequently Asked Questions About Divorce* as well as the creator of a series of workshops and classes that highlight the principles outlined in the *Squeeze the Most Out of Your Money* book.

Prior to establishing PS Worth, Patricia worked in a management or advisory capacity with several organizations, including American Express Financial Advisors, the University of Georgia, and Deloitte & Touche. She is also a former instructor in the Certified Financial Planner™ (CFP®) and Certified Divorce Financial Analysts (CDFA) programs at Oglethorpe University and columnist for the Atlanta Tribune.

Patricia is based in the Atlanta metro area. You can contact her at ps@psworth.com.

www.ingramcontent.com/pod-product-compliance
Lightning Source LLC
Chambersburg PA
CBHW060330200326
41519CB00011BA/1891
9780978550271